BOOMER SPIRITUALITY

BOOMER SPIRITUALITY

Seven Values for the Second Half of Life

CRAIG KENNET MILLER

DISCIPLESHIP
RESOURCES

ISBNs
978-0-88177-781-9 (print)
978-0-88177-782-6 (mobi)
978-0-88177-783-3 (ePub)

Library of Congress Control Number: 2016950119

DR781

For Ivy

Contents

Acknowledgments

To my father who said I could do anything I set my mind to do . . .

To my mother who taught me to always have faith . . .

To Connie and Dick, and Peggy and Bill, who have been constant companions on this journey . . .

To my fellow boomers, Rudy Rasmus, Duane Anders, Rob Huckaby, Dottie Escobedo-Frank, Linda McCoy, Tyrone Gordon, Bau Dang, Joe Daniels, and Vance Ross, for your prodding and support . . .

To countless pastors, teachers, and laypeople who have shared their insights . . .

To my colleagues at Discipleship Ministries who surround me with a culture of creativity grounded in discipleship . . .

To Joey Crowe, Lauren Ward, Cheryl Capshaw, Connie Schmutz, MaryJane Pierce Norton, Ken Sloane, and Will Randolph for editing and producing this book . . .

To my wife, Ivy, who never ceases to amaze me . . .

To my daughter, Jasmine, my son-in-law, Christopher, and my son, Matthew, who give me hope for the future . . .

I say thank you.

Introduction

Change can happen as the result of sudden events, like Pearl Harbor or 9/11, which can turn history on a dime and set the forces of culture in a new direction. Or change can happen as the result of political decisions lived into over time—like the evolving history of the United States since its birth as a nation or the Chinese revolution of Mao that shaped the lives of more than a billion people since 1949.

The change we are talking about in this book—demographic change—is different. Demographic change comes with a timeline that gives us a past, the present, and a presumed future of a generation. As the result of a high birth rate in the United States from 1946 to 1964, the baby boomer generation has had an impact on every phase of life.

Born after World War II, boomers have made their mark on each stage of the life span by virtue of their sheer numbers. Whether it was scooping up coonskin hats, hula hoops, and Barbie dolls when they were children, or embracing the ethos of rock 'n' roll when they were teenagers, or getting in on the housing boom of the 1990s, this generation has long asserted its influence on the American culture.

Boomers are now in the second half of life (age fifty and older). Because of longer life spans, more people are living into their eighties and nineties. Some will live past one hundred.

In 2020, the oldest boomer will turn seventy-four years old, while the youngest will turn fifty-six. By 2035 the oldest boomer will be eighty-nine and the youngest will be seventy-one.

At first glance, this may not seem to be a big deal—until you do the math. From now until 2029, ten thousand boomers will retire every day. The number of people over the age of sixty-five in the United States will grow from 56 million in 2020 to 79 million in 2035. By 2050, the number of adults in the U.S. over the age of sixty-five will increase to more than 89 million. Even more startling, the number of oldest old, those over eighty-five, will go from 7 million in 2020 to 19 million in 2050, almost tripling the number of those who will need the most care.[1]

It's hard to understand the implications of these numbers. At no time in history has there been such a large number of people over sixty-five years of age actively engaged in life.

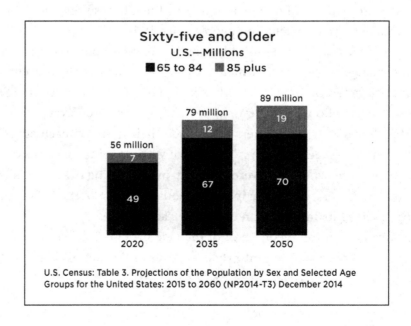

U.S. Census: Table 3. Projections of the Population by Sex and Selected Age Groups for the United States: 2015 to 2060 (NP2014-T3) December 2014

Because of scientific breakthroughs in medical technology, food preparation, and health care, people are living longer, much longer. While we may laugh at statements like "sixty is the new fifty," the second half of life for boomers will be much different from that of previous generations.

The reality is our society is ill-prepared for the demographic wave that is coming our way. The idea that retirement is a reward for work well done is long over. The concept of the endless vacation free of responsibility is just not feasible for most people. The image of a walled oasis of golf, swimming, and frequent trips to the local casino is not a reality for most of those approaching retirement age.

Recently, I was at meeting with a group of pastors and leaders. The chair of the meeting had been retired for about six months. Before retirement, she served in a leadership position in her denomination. She had responsibility for managing a group of staff plus putting together programs and training for hundreds of pastors and laity.

Suddenly in the middle of the meeting, she broke down in tears: "You don't know what it's like out there. My church and the senior center treat us like we are mindless infants with nothing to do."

She explained that the goal of the older-adult ministries at her church and the senior center in her community was to keep people entertained and give them something to do with their time. "They don't recognize us for what we can offer, for the people we are. I'm not dead yet!"

This vibrant, talented, and experienced woman had run headfirst into a world that was designed for the senior life of years past. When she is 85, maybe this is what she will need. But now, she needs to be challenged, to have opportunities to serve, and to be valued.

Boomers have always wanted to make a difference in the world. And in many ways they have. Bill Gates, Steve Jobs, Bill Clinton, Hillary Clinton, George W. Bush, Barack Obama, Donald Trump, Steven Spielberg, Meryl Streep, Tom Hanks, and Oprah Winfrey are just some of the names that crop up when we think of boomers.

Some might think that as boomers head toward their older-adult years, their time is past. Nothing could be further from the truth. Whether it's in the business world, the political world, the religious world, or the entertainment world, boomers will still make their mark.

In fact, we are on the verge of transforming what it means to be over sixty. In the coming decades, some aspects of older age will get better, especially in the arena of medical advances, the use of digital technology to connect with family and friends, and the convenience of businesses that bring goods and services directly to the home.

But other aspects of aging are going to prove daunting. The boomers who have managed their finances well, who have saved for their retirement years, who have developed a network of supportive friends and family, who see their lives as having purpose and meaning will enjoy a golden age unlike any generation before them.

But the boomers who have not been able to save, who lost jobs during the Great Recession, who live with broken relationships, and who are totally dependent on government services such as Social Security and Medicare are a different story. Their financial, medical, housing, social, and spiritual needs will affect every aspect of American society well into the future.

In the pages that follow, I invite you to think about the spiritual values of the boomer generation. I have been wrestling with this topic since I wrote my dissertation on boomer spirituality way back in the early 1990s. My first book, *Baby Boomer Spirituality: Ten Essential Values of a Generation,* looked at members of the boomer generation as they were in midlife, when they were raising children, creating businesses, taking the lead in politics, and shaping the culture. Twenty-four years later, the world is a different place. The digital revolution has changed the way we live. What we understood to be "truth" in 1992 we now view in a different light. Boomers are now at the forefront of creating what it means to be "old" in the twenty-first century.

As much as we would like to think that people change their values over time, it would be more accurate to say generations are shaped by the experiences and events of their childhood and youth. These experiences and events turn into ideals that stay with a generation throughout its life. Now that boomers are entering their postwork life, they are returning to the values of their youth.

Boomer Spirituality invites you to explore the values of *brokenness, loneliness, rootlessness,* and *self-seeking* that form the spiritual roots of boomers. Born out of the crucible of the 1960s and 1970s, these values still inform boomers' relationships with society and with the people around them. Many of the rancorous debates we see in our political sphere are the result of unresolved issues between first-wave boomers who embraced the counterculture as young adults and those who held on to the values of their parents' generation.

Godliness, supernaturalism, and *wholeness* capture the boomers' unique search for God as they look toward a future that is filled with peril and promise. The heated debates in Christian denominations over cultural issues find their beginnings in the religious revolts of the 1970s and 1980s, when a large portion of boomers gravitated to the new age movement or eschewed the traditional mainline churches in favor of the nondenominational megachurches that now dominate the American religious scene.

As boomers age, these issues will not suddenly disappear. They will be amplified as younger generations wrestle with how to take care of an aging generation who wants to stay young, who relishes its freedom, and whose rampant individualism has led to broken relationships and diminished financial resources.

As a boomer, I come to this analysis with a particular perspective. I am blessed to be married and to have one child in her twenties and another in his teens. As a United Methodist pastor, I have served in a denominational position that has offered me the opportunity to travel and interact with people around the world. Raised in California, I have lived in Nashville for more than twenty years. My mom is in her late nineties, and my two older sisters and their families are a major influence in my life, as are my wife's mother and siblings. If you want to pin me down as an evangelical or a liberal, good luck. I am still trying to figure it out.

So what follows are the personal musings of a boomer that are part history, part cultural commentary, and part spiritual insight. It is my hope that you will also find a thread of conviction that runs throughout the book—God stills love us.

If you are a boomer, you are sure to be reminded of the events and experiences that had an impact on you when you were young. If you are the child or grandchild of a boomer, perhaps this book will help you understand why your parents or grandparents act the way they do. If you are creating ministry for this generation, then this will be a guide to the way boomers view the world and look toward the future.

PART
1

Spiritual Roots

Over the Rainbow

Somewhere over the rainbow blue-birds fly....
If happy little blue-birds fly beyond the rainbow, Why, oh why can't I?

CHAPTER
1

Brokenness

Two images stand out clearly in my mind when I think of the 1960s.

The first is the image of my father and me, standing in a long line at the grocery store with three carts filled with canned food and paper goods; it was during the height of the Cuban Missile Crisis in the fall of 1962.

All day my father had hammered plywood over the windows in the basement of our house and had stored water in a trash can in the expectation of a nuclear attack. I remember helping him look at the plywood that covered the windows to see if there were any cracks where radiation might seep through if we were hit. It was the first time I had seen him scared. At the grocery store, I realized we were not alone in our fear. All around us were anxious people with shopping carts filled with survival goods. At eight years old, I felt fearful of the future for the first time.

The second image was looking at my reel-to-reel tape recorder as I listened to an audio letter sent to me by Norman, a family friend. In the late 1960s, he was deployed to Vietnam with the Navy. During his time there, we would exchange tapes. As a young teen, I found the signs of the war hard to miss. There were the images on TV and the whispered anxiety in my older sister's voice as she dealt with the issues of her friends trying to avoid the draft. Norman's audio letters to me were a direct link to a war that was dividing the nation. I distinctly remember one tape on which I heard a helicopter taking off in the background as he said, "It's time to go." I would play that tape over and over again to see if I could hear any other sounds of war.

Like pictures flashing in a psychedelic movie, other images of the '60s and early '70s cloud my memories: John John saluting his father's coffin in the East Room of the White House . . . body bags being lifted off a helicopter in Vietnam . . . Tiny Tim singing "Tiptoe through the Tulips" on *Laugh In* . . . Neil Armstrong stepping onto the moon saying, "One small step for a man, one giant leap for mankind."

Martin Luther King Jr. proclaiming, "I have a dream" . . . King's body on a hotel balcony in Memphis, Tennessee . . . The Beatles singing "I Want to Hold Your Hand" on *The Ed Sullivan Show* . . . Woodstock, hippies, miniskirts, and love beads.

Fires raging during the Watts riots . . . the police chief of Saigon blowing out the brains of a Viet Cong officer with a pistol shot . . . President Johnson holding his dog up by the ears . . . police officers and demonstrators confronting one another outside the Democratic Convention in Chicago . . . Jane Fonda perched behind an antiaircraft gun in Hanoi.

Tommy Smith and John Carlos raising their fists in a Black Power salute on the victory stand at the Olympics as "The Star-Spangled Banner" was being played . . . Bobby Kennedy giving a victory salute at the Ambassador Hotel in Los Angeles . . . Bobby Kennedy's head being held after he was shot in a dark kitchen passageway.

Charles Manson in handcuffs . . . Hare Krishnas at the airport . . . the bodies of students at Kent State . . . John and Yoko at a bed-in for peace . . . Patty Hearst holding a rifle in front of a Symbionese Liberation banner . . . Richard Nixon boarding a helicopter after resigning from the presidency.

For me, these are not just pictures in a history book—they are part of my childhood. Like playing football with my friends on the street, going to school, and dressing up to go to church on Sundays, these events shaped my understanding of the world and my outlook on life itself.

It was a crazy time to grow up. For me, "normal" was sitting in front of the TV with the family at dinner and watching the body counts from Vietnam being reported like scores in a basketball game on the evening news: Americans, 10; Viet Cong, 230. It was the only game I knew where the winners tried to come up with the lowest score.

Normal was watching race riots in major cities and seeing police officers swinging clubs at black clergymen. It was seeing women burning their bras in protest against a male-dominated society. It was watching the draft lottery on TV like it was a game show, with the winners getting an all-expenses-paid trip to Vietnam, courtesy of the U.S. Army. It was challenging authority at every turn and believing that everyone over thirty was against us and trying to wipe us out.

Regardless of politics and religion and ethical dilemmas, it was the boomers who went off and died in Vietnam. It was boomers who protested and burned draft cards. It was boomers who joined the throngs of civil rights activists. And it was boomers who were hit by the full impact of these events as they were coming of age.

When the World Began to Change

My mom says the world started to change when the Beatles appeared on *The Ed Sullivan Show* on February 9, 1964. She remembers the shock she felt when she saw the long hair and heard the hard beat of "I Want to Hold Your Hand." She was not alone. Seventy-three million Americans watched *The Ed Sullivan Show*. Sullivan himself had 50,000 ticket requests for a theater that housed only 700 people. In the month preceding the Beatles' appearance, their first single released in America sold two million copies, an unprecedented number of sales for the record industry.[1]

The Beatles are considered by some to be the best rock musicians ever. Combining the rhythm of American black music and the unique harmonies of John Lennon and Paul McCartney, they were a music force unequaled in the decade of the '60s. As talented as they were, much of their success had to do with timing. When the Beatles burst on the scene in January and February 1964, America was in the throes of a deep depression, not economic but psychological and spiritual. Two months earlier, on November 22, 1963, the country had been rocked by the devastating news that the president, John F. Kennedy, had been shot in Dallas as he was riding in an open convertible limousine in Dealey Plaza.

From Friday afternoon till the funeral service on Monday, the three major television networks gave complete, uninterrupted coverage to the incidents following the assassination. It was the most watched and most covered event of its time. People fifty-five and older still rank it as one of the most memorable moments in TV, right behind the coverage of 9/11.[2]

In the midst of that coverage, an improbable scene took place. On Sunday morning, as millions of Americans were watching live news coverage of Lee Harvey Oswald's transfer to the Dallas County jail, Oswald was shot and killed by Jack Ruby.

That event, even more than the assassination of Kennedy, began to sow seeds of doubt in America's conscience. How was it that Jack Ruby was able to kill Oswald while he was in police custody? Was Ruby acting alone or was he trying to cover up a conspiracy? Why was Oswald silenced? What key did he hold to the assassination of one of America's most popular presidents?

On September 24, 1964, ten months after Kennedy's death, the President's Commission on the Assassination of President Kennedy, known as the Warren Commission, presented its final report to President Lyndon B. Johnson. The report contained 888 pages and included 6,710 footnotes. Along with twenty-six supporting volumes that were released at a later date, the Warren Commission presented the American public with a staggering 20,000 pages of material, containing an amazing 10 million words. Its conclusions were simple:

- Lee Harvey Oswald, acting alone, killed Kennedy.
- Jack Ruby, acting alone, killed Oswald.
- There was no credible evidence of a conspiracy, foreign or domestic.
- Only three shots were fired, all from the Texas School Book Depository Building. One of these bullets passed through Kennedy's neck and then probably through the chest and wrist of Governor Connally. Another shot hit Kennedy's head. Another shot missed.[3]

As convincing as the arguments seemed, Americans were not impressed. After seeing the actual footage of the assassination, and after reading numerous books and seeing various TV news reports on the subject, most people did not trust the conclusions of the Warren Commission. In the lead up to the fiftieth anniversary of the assassination in 2013, 61 percent did not believe Oswald acted alone. At one time, in 1976, over 81 percent believed Kennedy was killed by conspirators.[4]

Broken Trust

Kurt Anderson, in an article in *Rolling Stone* in 1992, sums up his generation's view of life in this way:

> Nowadays, there are two sides to every answer. We don't face facts and, hell, simply decide. No. That would be too instinctual, too easy, too blithe, too unlike us. Instead we consider every alternative and feel complete enthusiasm for none of them. We postpone. We fret. We second-guess. . . . As individuals, and even as a nation, we grow faint at the prospect of absolute commitment, whether it's marriage, or military intervention in the third world, or thirty-year fixed-rate mortgages. . . .
>
> To most of us, every city, every book, practically every way of life is an interesting place to visit, but we wouldn't want to live there. Would we? Ours is a generation comfortably adrift, bobbing on a sea of ambivalence.[5]

What Anderson calls ambivalence, I call brokenness. It is a feeling that nothing and no one can be trusted, especially oneself. It is a feeling of continually being lost, not believing there is anything to find. It is like trying to walk in the surf at the ocean, with your feet madly trying to find a foothold, but continually slipping off slimy rocks and falling into shifting sand as the waves of change bombard you in a swirl of white foam.

It is living with the conviction that the trust you had in society has been violated. Discovering that the big promise of the American dream offered to you in your childhood turned out to be a broken series of lies, you feel betrayed. Growing up with a belief in all the so-called institutions of society—church, government, education, work, marriage, and family—you feel they have failed you miserably, leaving you totally alone in an uncaring and coldhearted world.

In childhood, baby boomers were raised with a set of assumptions about the world in which they lived.

First, they were Americans, citizens of the greatest, most powerful, most generous, and most giving nation on this earth.

Second, anyone could make it in America if one worked hard enough. Along with this was the firm belief that anyone could become president of the United States.

Third, America's political and economic system was the best in the world, and we must protect ourselves from the communists.

Fourth, military might would protect us as well as enable us to spread our values throughout the world.

Fifth, the traditional nuclear family of father, mother, and children, with father the breadwinner and mother the housewife, was ordained by God as the norm for all.

Sixth, we had unlimited natural resources and land at our disposal to use as we wished.

Seventh, technology and scientific breakthroughs would provide us with a boundless future and solve all our problems.

Eighth, only America and Russia counted. The rest of the world was divided into spheres of influence, and small countries provided no threat to our superiority.

Ninth, minorities should stay in their place, and the occasional accomplishments of a few of them were a deviation from the norm.

Tenth, by staying in line with what their parents dictated, and through education, the boomer generation would have a better life than their parents had, with no depressions, no wars, and all the consumer goods they would ever want.[6]

Furthermore, everyone knew that assassinations took place only in banana republics where despots and revolutionaries took power by force. Only in America was the power to rule passed on peacefully from president to president every four years. But from 1960 to 1980, only one president, Jimmy Carter, served a standard four-year term of office. Kennedy lasted three years; Johnson served five; Nixon, six; and Ford, two.

While President Kennedy's assassination had an impact on all of American society, Tom Shachtman, in *Decade of Shocks*, points out that the assassination affected children and adolescents the most. On the one hand, children identified the president as the most important symbol and leader of the government. To them, the president was almost a god-like figure. As a result of those perceptions, Kennedy's death was a threat to their security.

Presidential Terms from 1960 to 1980		
John F. Kennedy	1960–1963	Assassinated
Lyndon B. Johnson	1963–1969	Kennedy's vice president. He completed Kennedy's term of office and was elected to one term.
Richard Nixon	1969–1974	Nixon was impeached, and he resigned from office.
Gerald Ford	1974–1977	Nixon's vice president. He completed Nixon's term of office.
Jimmy Carter	1977–1981	Served four years

On the other hand, adolescents were attracted to the youthful and vigorous image of a president who could do no wrong. Because he was killed in his prime in a bloody spectacle before their eyes, their feelings of loss persisted long after the event took place.[7]

But the assassination of the president was just the beginning. The children and adolescents of the time, those boomers who still have a memory of what happened, are the ones who felt the strongest impact of the shots fired in Dealey Plaza. This was just the beginning of a series of events that would shape their future and their view of themselves.

Boomers Are Not All Alike

While the term *boomers* is a convenient word to use to describe those born from 1946 to 1964, they did not all experience the changes of the 1960s the same way. Depending on when they were born, the assassination of President Kennedy and the ensuing events of the sixties had a different impact. The group that felt the strongest effects was the "first-wave" boomers, those born between 1946 and 1952. The leading edge of this generation, who were born in 1946, were seniors in high school when President Kennedy was killed and were seniors in college when Martin Luther King Jr. and Robert Kennedy were assassinated. In 1974, when Nixon resigned, they were still two years shy of their thirtieth birthdays during a time when the future was up for grabs.

The Three Waves of the Boomers		
First-Wave Boomers	**Second-Wave Boomers**	**Third-Wave Boomers**
Born 1946–1952	**Born 1953–1958**	**1959–1964**
Were high school seniors when President Kennedy was assassinated and college seniors when Martin Luther King Jr. and Robert Kennedy were assassinated.	Were children when Kennedy was assassinated and in middle school when Martin Luther King Jr. and Robert Kennedy were assassinated.	Have little or no memory of President Kennedy's assassination and were children in 1968.
Men of this wave were subjugated to the draft lottery in 1969, when men born from 1944–1952 were drafted into the military by a lottery based on their date of birth. More than 2.5 million served in Vietnam.	These *Wonder Years* kids saw older siblings and neighbors go off to Vietnam and participate in protests against the war and in favor of civil rights. They were the ones asked to get under their desks at school in case of a nuclear attack. The draft lottery was discontinued before they were drafted.	By 1973 Americans had withdrawn from Vietnam, so these boomers were not personally involved in the conflict over the war. They were much more influenced by the ongoing Cold War between Russia and the United States and the threat of nuclear war.
Were divided between those who embraced the counterculture and those who held on to the values of their parents. This divide is still seen in the political battles between the Right and the Left, which leaves little room for a middle ground.	Raised on reruns of *The Twilight Zone, The Outer Limits,* and *Star Trek*, many in this group became the leaders of the digital age and created the first personal computers and software that now fuel the economy.	This group had to adapt to the changing patterns of childhood, as a large percentage of their parents went through divorce. The cultural norms of the 1950s were replaced by the uncertainty of a 1960s culture that was in disarray.

They truly were the Woodstock generation. Their adolescence and young adulthood was rocked by transformation and change. In an article in *Business Month*, Aimee I. Stern helps us see the radical changes first-wave boomers felt as they were growing up.

Jane . . . was born in the first wave of the baby boom. In the year she began college, life was arranged into a series of cubicles. Mom stayed home and defined herself through roast beef. Dad went to work and supported his family. Jane wasn't sure she would finish college. No matter. She would meet the man of her dreams, get married, buy a house and have a mortgage and children.

At college, rules were rigid. Men couldn't go upstairs in the dorm even during the day without signing in, and the dorm mother conducted a bed check every night. Three years later men and women lived together in that same dorm. Vietnam took the lives of some of Jane's friends, and her school went wild in protest. In the year that Jane got out of school, the world was a very different place.[8]

By the mid-1970s these boomers were dubbed the "Me Generation"; and by the 1980s, the more affluent were the frontrunners of the "yuppies" (young, upwardly mobile professionals).

In the 1990s, Bill Clinton became the first boomer president. Born in 1946, he fully embraced the ethos of the progressive first-wave boomers. As a bigger-than-life character, he protested against the Vietnam War when he was a Rhodes scholar in England, admitted to trying marijuana but didn't inhale, and embraced the Democratic party's values. In his campaign, Clinton featured a picture of himself as a high school student shaking hands with President Kennedy in 1963, just months before Kennedy's assassination.

As president, Clinton worked with a Republican Congress to institute a number of reforms that led to a decade of economic gains, highlighted by the emergence of the World Wide Web. Even though there was a dotcom bust on Wall Street in March of 2000, the potential of the Internet was unleashed into the lives of everyday Americans.

In the 2000s, when George W. Bush was president, boomers witnessed major disruptions in the economy, the growth of the digital world, and the fragmentation of the old world order as terrorism in all its various forms led to war and a general feeling of unease.

George W., who also was born in 1946, represents a different side of the first-wave boomers, those who wished to retain the traditional American values that were challenged by the radicals of the 1960s. During the Vietnam War, he served in the Texas National Guard but was never deployed to Vietnam. He confessed to abusing alcohol, but his life was turned around by his faith in Jesus Christ. He called himself a compassionate conservative and promised to restore dignity to the office after the Monica Lewinsky scandal that rocked Clinton late in his second term.

The byplay between the progressive and traditional first-wave boomers has dominated the political scene since the election of Bill Clinton. As a result, we have a deadlocked political system with one side fighting against the other. There are red states and blue state, pro-lifers and pro-choicers, pro-gay and anti-gay, those in favor of traditional marriage and those in favor of same sex-marriage, and the list goes on and on.

In a real sense, these political battles are the result of the unresolved conflicts from the experiences of first-wavers in the sixties. While the iconic image of the sixties is the Vietnam protester wearing a peace sign and love beads at Woodstock, the majority of boomers served in Vietnam, never dropped out of society to join a commune, went to work, and formed households that fueled the economic booms and busts of the 1980s, 1990s, and 2000s.

By virtue of being first, the first-wave boomers had advantages over the younger boomers. After finishing high school and college, they were able to find work, form families, and gain a foothold in the economy. *Business Month* identified them as the group that "became prosperous quickly, grabbing the best jobs and getting in on the housing boom."[9]

This luck of the draw will continue as they live into their seventies and move into the next phase of their life span. Like the older adults before them, they will still get the full benefits of Social Security and Medicare. Most of them weathered the effects of the Great Recession of 2008 and since then have been beneficiaries of the growth of the stock market and the rise in housing prices. Most of those who sent their children to college did so before the escalation of college tuition started in 2000.

Second- and Third-Wave Boomers

The "second-wave" boomers, those born between 1953 and 1958, were still young enough to adapt to the changes that their older brothers and sisters saw as threats or revelations. Though confused and impressed by the counterculture, feminism, drugs, free sex, and protests against the war, second wavers had more resiliency by virtue of being youthful teenagers.

When they were in their early twenties, they were the first to seize new opportunities generated by scientific advances in computer technology. Steven Jobs and Bill Gates are the poster children for second-wave boomers. They created the dynamic changes in technology that now are essential to everyday living. Apple and Microsoft were born in the midst of a revolutionary time when what seemed impossible came to fruition. Jobs, Gates, and their fellow travelers were the creators of personal digital devices that have transformed virtually every aspect of our lives.

Third-wave boomers, born between 1959 and 1964, who barely remember many of the startling events of the '60s, are far more likely to have faced disillusionment as a result of downward mobility. Rather than facing social and political change, younger boomers have faced economic loss.

For this third wave of boomers, the sexual revolution came to a crashing halt when the AIDS crisis hit the young during the early 1980s. Sexual experimentation put many of them at risk as they navigated a dating world whose most pressing question was whether your date was AIDS-free.

When Barack Obama, a third-wave boomer, came into the presidency in 2009, his slogan, "Change We Can Believe In," echoed the sentiments of his age cohort, whose hopes were being battered by economic loss and social unrest. For them, change in the past had not led to greater prosperity, but a loss of trust in government and in the financial institutions that undergirded the economy.

The America that Donald Trump will lead as president beginning in 2017 is one that is much different from the America of his predecessors. As a first-wave boomer, Trump will face great challenges that have been building since Bill Clinton served as the first boomer president. The cultural divide between liberals and conservatives, addressing racial injustice in the police and justice systems, taking care of the old and the young, and the menace of terrorism are all issues that have been growing over the years. Perhaps the most daunting is the disparity of the economic system that increasingly divides the rich and the poor and deeply affects the economic future of boomers and their children.

The Great Recession's Impact on Boomers and Their Children

For boomers, the economic success of their parents' generation was built on a middle-class lifestyle where a family headed by a working father and a mother at home was the norm. As boomers moved into adulthood, they realized it took two incomes to maintain the middle-class lifestyle.

The Great Recession (December 2007–June 2009) dealt a deathblow to many boomers' dreams of doing better than their parents' generation. In 2007, middle-class

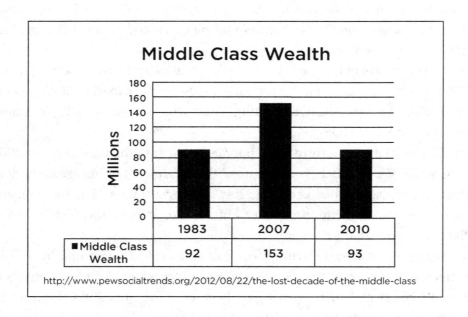

Middle Class Wealth

	1983	2007	2010
■ Middle Class Wealth	92	153	93

Millions

http://www.pewsocialtrends.org/2012/08/22/the-lost-decade-of-the-middle-class

household wealth had reached $157,000. By 2010, it had dropped to just over $93,000, barely $1,000 over the same measure in 1983.[10]

The breakdown in the economic system had an even greater negative impact on the children of boomers. People ages thirty-five to forty-four lost 44 percent of their net worth and those under thirty-four lost 68 percent compared to people their age in 1983.

School debt, a downsizing of middle-class jobs, and a loss of high paying jobs has translated into a bleak economic picture for today's young adults. Those who went to college are challenged by school debt. Two-thirds of recent graduates owe more than $26,000. Added together, recent college graduates have wracked up more than $1.2 trillion in debt.[11]

In 2015, the U.S. Census produced a report that showed the difference between the young adulthood of boomers in 1980 and the young adulthood of millennials in 2013. While 22.9 percent of boomers lived with a parent in 1980, 30.3 percent of millennials did so in 2013. In 1980, 18.9 percent of boomer women who were mothers were unmarried. In 2013, 40.6 percent of millennial women who had children were unmarried. The number of those who were never married had grown from 41.5 percent in 1980 to 65.9 percent by 2013. The number of young adults who were living in poverty increased from 14.1 percent in 1980 to 19.7 percent in 2013.[12]

Boomers, especially those buffeted by the economic peaks and busts of the last twenty years, find themselves in an untenable situation. While they know they should be saving for their retirement, they are focused on getting through the next day. They are also faced with a sad realization: their children will find it almost impossible to afford the lifestyles they have been able to obtain.

This is especially true of boomers and their children who live in large cities such as Los Angeles, Washington, D.C., and New York City. To rent an average apartment in Los Angeles County, a person needs to make $33 an hour or $68,640 a year. This is well above the $15 an hour many groups are advocating as a minimum wage. If you want to buy a house, your income needs to increase to more than $96,000 a year to afford the average house that costs more than $560,000.[13]

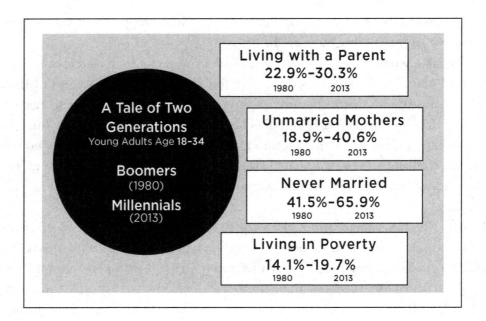

A Tale of Two Generations
Young Adults Age 18-34

Boomers
(1980)
Millennials
(2013)

Living with a Parent
22.9%–30.3%
1980   2013

Unmarried Mothers
18.9%–40.6%
1980   2013

Never Married
41.5%–65.9%
1980   2013

Living in Poverty
14.1%–19.7%
1980   2013

Less-Educated Boomers Are Projected to Have Shorter Life Spans Than Their Parents

Many boomers are facing something quite unforeseen: they will have shorter lifespans than their parents. Researchers Anne Case and Angus Deaton discovered a surprising rise in death rates among middle-aged white non-Hispanics whose number of deaths are akin to the AIDS crises of the early 1980s. The main culprits of this epidemic are increasing death rates from drug overdoes, suicide, and cirrhosis, mainly attributed to alcoholism.

This trend is especially pronounced among less educated whites who reported declines in health, the ability to do daily activities, and keeping a job. High among this list was chronic pain, which led many to opiate addictions. One of the chief causes has been their lowered economic prospects and loss of jobs due to the demise of manufacturing jobs across the country. While the more affluent saw losses in their stock portfolios, the middle-income and the poor lost the ability to find a job.

The authors of the report stated, "Although the epidemic of pain, suicide, and drug overdoses preceded the financial crisis, ties to economic insecurity are possible. After the productivity slowdown in the early 1970s, and with widening income inequality, many of the baby-boom generation are the first to find, in midlife, that they will not be better off than were their parents."[14]

This startling trend is a reminder that as boomers age, many will be challenged by illnesses and addictions that will cut short their lives. Churches and nonprofits that are willing to embrace ministry with boomers will be critical providers of support for boomers and their families as they face an uncertain future.

Boomers as the Breadbasket for Their Extended Families

In the midst of these stark economic realities, a majority of boomers with children or elderly parents have become the breadbasket for their extended families. Ironically, those who have been the most responsible with their money are the ones giving the most financial support to their families.

Sixty-eight percent of people age fifty and over have provided financial support to their children without expecting anything in return. Twenty-six percent have done so for grandchildren; 16 percent, for their parents; 13 percent, for siblings; and 14 percent, for other family members. This generosity comes at a cost. Instead of saving for their retirement, they are providing for their children, grandchildren, and extended families.[15]

Critics of the boomers, like Anya Kamenetz in *Generation Debt*, blame boomers for living beyond their means and have little sympathy for their financial predicament. Kamenetz says, "Instead of saving enough for their retirement, let alone for our future, the boomers are going into deeper debt than any generation before them. Because of their projected retirement expenses, the entire nation is essentially bankrupt, with a total accumulated funding gap in the federal budget that's greater than our net worth. Who's going to be around when that bill comes due? Young people."[16]

Boomers also know the forecast for the future has its downsides. If no changes are made in Social Security, benefits will have to cut by 23 percent by 2033 for the system to stay solvent. This is especially troubling for the 36 percent of boomers who see Social Security as their main source of income.[17]

The Legacy of the Vietnam War

Ironically, the largest demographic group ever seen in America, 75 million strong, the group to whom parents held out such promise, is the same group that is heading into retirement years wondering what happened to the American dream of their youth. This disillusionment with the future is deeply connected to the gut-wrenching events of 1963 to 1974, events that caused America to ask how much more it could take.

The most influential event of them all was the Vietnam War. The soldiers of Vietnam were the youngest to ever leave our shores. They fought and died at an average age of twenty-three, three years younger than those who served in World War II and five years younger than those who served in the Persian Gulf War and the wars in Iraq and Afghanistan.

The people who served in Vietnam were from the common stock of America, men like Joey Sintoni, who grew up in Sagamore, Massachusetts. After joining the army, Joey served as part of the honor guard for funerals at Arlington National Cemetery. Realizing that the men who were dying in Vietnam were men his own age, he volunteered to serve in Vietnam. In January 1968 he was stationed in the Mekong Delta area near the Cambodian border. When he arrived, he unfurled a large American flag and attached it to a tank. After a few weeks of battle, his flag, which he had brought with him from Arlington, was burnt up when a rocket hit the tank. Of the flag, he wrote, "It flew proudly to its hot death."

Joey went to Vietnam with high expectations of fighting for a noble cause and of defending America. But after two months of battle, he was the only one of a group of twelve men who was alive or able to fight. In his diary he wrote:

> I am not trying to be a fatalist, but I realize I'll never be able to make one year alive in the field, unless the fighting drastically changes or the war ends, both of which are unlikely. The "oldest" guy in my platoon, one still in the field, still

able to fight, has been here six and a half months. All of a sudden I realize I may never see the woman or family my heart beats for. I dare not make a friend.[18]

Nineteen days later, Joey was dead. Before his death, Joey wrote a letter to his girlfriend, Angela, which was to be delivered to her in case he died. His devotion to his country is expressed in these words:

Vietnam is a test of the American spirit. I hope I have helped in a little way to pass the test. The press, the television screen, the magazines are filled with the images of young men burning their draft cards to demonstrate their courage. Their rejection is of the ancient law that a male fights to protect his own people and his own land.

Does it take courage to flaunt the authorities and burn a draft card? Ask the men at Dak To, Con Tien, or Hill 875, they'll tell you how much courage it takes.

Most people never think of their freedom. . . . Why must people take their freedom for granted? Why can't they support the men who are trying to protect their lifeblood, freedom?

I've died as I've always hoped, protecting what I hold dear to my heart. We will meet again in the future. We will. I'll be waiting for that day.

The inevitable, well, the last one: I love you with all my heart and my love for you will survive into eternity.

Your Joey[19]

The story does not end there. Joey's death, like all the deaths in Vietnam, sent waves of grief and confusion through family and friends. After hearing the news of Joey's death, Angela's dreams for the future went up in smoke. They had already picked out the names for their children who would fill their two-story dream house overlooking the Cape Cod Canal. She said after Joey's death: "I lost that dream. When he died, I just didn't pick up the pieces and go out and find some boyfriend I could marry. I was supposed to marry Joey Sintoni. I didn't find it easy to progress to Plan B. Marriage was killed in action."

Eight days after Joey died, Martin Luther King Jr. was gunned down, and two months later Robert Kennedy was assassinated. Angela's world was on fire. Of her feelings, she said: "I had that sense of futility, of what's the use. It took a long time for me to care again and feel hopeful. . . . It made me old real fast."[20]

The death of Joey was also the death of Angela's dreams, an experience shared by millions of this generation. The boomers who burned draft cards and protested in the streets did so not out of disrespect or because they were unpatriotic; they did so because they knew something was terribly wrong. The generation that as children had said the Pledge of Allegiance with eyes focused on the American flag in schoolhouses across the nation now questioned all that it stood for.

"I pledge allegiance to the flag of the United States of America." How could you pledge allegiance to a flag under whose banner your brothers, friends, and lovers were being slaughtered by the thousands in an undeclared war?

"And to the republic for which it stands, one nation under God." What kind of God would bless this kind of war in which the most powerful nation on earth would send two million of its young into a war that it had no desire of winning and whose strategic importance rested on the so-called domino theory?

"Indivisible, with liberty and justice for all" seemed to be a reality only for the wealthy and the politically connected who could keep their sons out of Vietnam.

Twenty years later boomers talked about their bitter disillusionment resulting from the war in Vietnam. *Rolling Stone*, in its landmark "Portrait of a Generation" survey published in 1988, reported that almost half of the baby boom generation had personal knowledge of the human losses in Vietnam. Forty-eight percent of all boomers and 70 percent of first-wave boomers knew someone—a friend, relative, or acquaintance—who was killed, missing, or wounded in Vietnam.[21]

Vietnam vets had an especially bitter pill to swallow; many returning home from the war were vilified by their peers. Flashbacks, suicide, Agent Orange, and homelessness affected many. Anger, hate, frustration, and low morale were the demons they have fought since coming home. Most vets felt abandoned by the ones they loved and by the country for which they had fought. They were the American warriors who were not welcomed home as heroes by their fellow Americans.

In contrast, the one constant theme of the Gulf War in 1990, the first war after Vietnam, was "we" were not going to do it again. Gulf War soldiers had America's full support; they were not rejected and ignored like their counterparts from the Vietnam War. Regardless of how we felt about war, we were not going to let the Gulf War soldiers be abandoned or forgotten. So Americans unfurled their red, white, and blue flags and tied yellow ribbons around trees, houses, and buildings. They wore yellow bows on their blouses and suits as if they were badges of honor. They sent videos, cards, cassette tapes, T-shirts, bubble gum, and brownies in shipments that flooded the military's capacity to carry them. They welcomed home the Gulf veterans with parades, speeches, and TV specials. All of this was done in a frenzy of activity that had more to do with unresolved guilt over Vietnam than with welcoming home the victors of the "One Hundred Hour War."

The most profound symbol and lasting remembrance of the 1960s experience is a black granite, V-shaped wall with the names of 58,272 veterans who died in the Vietnam War. The uniqueness of the Vietnam Veterans Memorial lies not in its shape, but in the polished surface of the black granite in which you can see your own reflection wavering over the names of those who gave their lives in Vietnam.

In many ways, it has become America's wailing wall. Since its dedication on November 11, 1982, it has become the most visited monument in Washington, D.C. Laura Palmer, the author of a moving book about people's experiences and remembrances of Vietnam, *Shrapnel in the Heart*, said of its dedication:

> It was then that America finally turned to embrace her own. Engraved on the wall's black granite panels that pry open the earth are the names of every man and woman who went to Vietnam and never returned. In dedicating the memorial, America finally acknowledged that we lost more than the war in Vietnam; we lost the warriors. The war was deplorable, not the men who served.[22]

As the Vietnam Veterans Memorial is the lasting symbol of the events of the '60s, the resulting spiritual root of the boomer generation is one of brokenness, a sense of loss and disillusionment over what happened to them and a clear break from the assumptions that guided their parents' generation. This sense of not being whole, of still trying to survive the turmoil of their youth, of living with unfulfilled expectations has produced three other spiritual realities in boomers: loneliness, rootlessness, and self-seeking, which play a part in the daily lives of the boomer generation.

CHAPTER
2

Loneliness

When my daughter left for college, my world was turned upside down. Because she was in Boston and I was in Nashville, I knew we would see little of her during the year. While she went to start a new phase of life, I was the one left behind. That is the irony children can't see. When they say they want to go away to college, that means they are leaving someone behind.

For six months, I groused around the house. My daughter played the piano and the violin; and with her gone, the music stopped in our house. I threw myself into a project, making a train layout in the basement with the Lionel trains I played with when I was a child. Ostensibly, this was for my elementary school-age son, but the reality is this was my way to deal with my loss.

The strange part is I wasn't alone: my wife and my son were in the house with me, but each of us was dealing with this new change in our own way. Now that I look back on that time, I realize that it wasn't depression or grief that beset me; it was loneliness. So much of my life had been wrapped around her activities, goals, and my dreams for her future. When the future arrived, I was ill-prepared.

It didn't make matters any easier that just before leaving for college, she recorded a CD of songs she had written while in high school. The last song on the CD was "All Grown Up," in which she shared the joy of her childhood, but said that she knew her life would never be the same. This chapter of her life was over. Of course, being the foolish father that I am, I listened to that song way too often as I drove to work. In those moments, I realized that a chapter of fatherhood was over for me as well.

Loneliness is somewhat of a constant companion for a large number of boomers. It's what drives boomer parents to become "helicopter parents," who intervene too frequently on their adult children's behalf. It's what drives them to reveal their daily lives on Facebook as they recount the meals they had that day and how many times they brushed their teeth. It's what keeps them on their phones talking and texting when they are driving.

For along with a sense of brokenness, boomers also carry within them a profound feeling of loneliness that is tied to how they form and discard relationships. In the aftermath of the tumultuous 1960s and 1970s, the following defined the changing nature of boomer relationships as they hit their thirties and forties:

Fifty percent of their marriages ended in divorce.[1]
Thirty percent lived together outside of marriage.[2]
Fourteen percent were pregnant outside of marriage.
Five percent had an abortion.[3]
Twenty-five percent of boomer women remained childless.[4]
Twenty-five percent had one child.[5]
Thirty-three percent were single.
Sixteen percent were single parents.
Twenty-six percent of them were in marriages where both husband and wife worked.[6]
Fewer than five percent lived in a traditional marriage where the husband worked and the wife stayed home with the children.

You would think that as the people of this generation moved into their fifties and sixties, these figures would change. But in 2014, these trends continued. Thirty-six percent of boomers in 2014 were single. This means over 25 million boomers are widowed, divorced, separated, or never married.[7]

These trends are also reflected in the living arrangements of adults. In 1967 when boomers were ages three to twenty-one, more than 70 percent of their parents and grandparents lived with a spouse. By 2016, when boomers were ages fifty to sixty-eight, just over 50 percent of adults lived with a spouse.

These facts point to something that gets overlooked when looking at this generation. Boomers have reconfigured what it means to be a family. To a boomer, a "family" could mean a number of options. A family could be a divorced man and a divorced woman living together in a trial marriage. A family could be a remarriage on the part of both husband and wife, each bringing along a couple of children, thus making a blended family. A family could be two gay men who are married with an adopted child, or a single parent with two children. A family may be a single mom with her twenty-something daughter and ninety-something mother living under the same roof. The descriptions of "family" are endless.

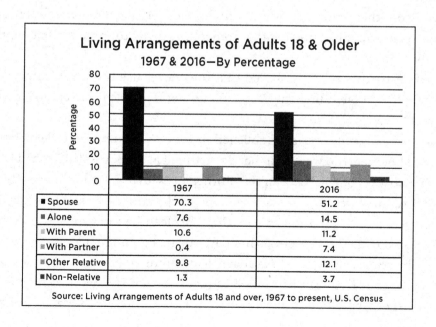

Living Arrangements of Adults 18 & Older
1967 & 2016—By Percentage

	1967	2016
■ Spouse	70.3	51.2
■ Alone	7.6	14.5
▨ With Parent	10.6	11.2
▨ With Partner	0.4	7.4
▨ Other Relative	9.8	12.1
■ Non-Relative	1.3	3.7

Source: Living Arrangements of Adults 18 and over, 1967 to present, U.S. Census

A New Definition of Family Challenges the Church

The institution of society that has been most affected by the shifting nature of family life is the church. Church is the unique place that celebrates family life. Weddings, baptisms, confirmations, and funerals are rites of passage designed to affirm and support families as they transition through different stages of life.

Churches of the 1950s and 1960s created ministries that were geared to support a traditional family with two parents who were married and had children. Churches saw themselves as an extension of family life where stable relationships nurtured children as they moved toward adulthood. Church leaders were fairly confident that if they provided meaningful worship and a consistent way of teaching children the beliefs of the Christian faith, enough people in the community would participate to support the various ministries of the church.

But as boomers entered adulthood, the traditional family went by the wayside. Perhaps the most devastating blow to congregations came as a result of key families going through divorce. Parents not only divorced each other; in many cases, they divorced themselves from their churches. Many who have experienced divorce find it too painful to show up in worship, knowing that someone is going to wonder what happened to their family.

A group of pastors recently shared that they never use the word "family" in their preaching for fear of offending one group or another if people felt excluded by whatever definition of "family" was being used.

In *The Postponed Generation*, published in 1987, Susan Littwin talked about Kathleen, a young boomer who worked in her department at school. Kathleen had told her in the fall that she was going to take an accounting job with a "big eight" firm after Christmas. But Christmas went by and spring came, and Kathleen was still in the office. In a casual conversation Susan discovered that Kathleen had not moved on to the "big eight" because during the Christmas holidays she had gotten married.

Since Christmas, Susan and Kathleen had innumerable conversations about all kinds of things, but Kathleen had failed to mention that she had just married, something her mother would have proclaimed in headlines in the newspaper. When Susan asked her why she had failed to mention her marriage, Kathleen and she had the following conversation.

"I don't know," Kathleen says in her soft voice, pushing the hair out of her very lovely blue eyes. "I just didn't want people to think I had changed or to act different toward me. When you're married, people expect you to act out a certain role, and I don't want a role. I just want to be myself. For instance, my father thinks I ought to be buying furniture and china now that we're married. I have no interest in any of that right now."

"Why did you get married? " I asked.

"Well, I was in this relationship, and I didn't know where it was going. He's going east in the summer, and wanted me to come with him, so he said, 'Let's get married,' and we did. But it doesn't really make anything different."[8]

Kathleen's attitude toward marriage was very different from that of her parents' generation. When her parents' generation got married, it was a lifelong commitment, made in the belief that people should stay together "for better, for worse, for richer, for poorer, in sickness and in health, till death do us part."[9]

But since the 1960s, the emphasis of relationships is no longer focused on commitment and sticking it out no matter what. Instead we have Kathleen's remark: "I just want to be myself."

In fact, for boomers like her, marriage is a controversial choice. For them, the norm is to float in and out of a series of relationships that last as long as they work out. More tellingly, marriage is just one possible lifestyle option in a world of confusing, changing relationships.

Boomers Are Still Divorcing

While we would like to think this is a phase that people grow out of as they age, the reality is that boomers are still leading the way when it comes to divorce and remarriage.

Demographers Sheela Kennedy and Steven Ruggles from the University of Minnesota discovered that while the divorce rate has flattened for the general population, not all generations are experiencing this. While younger people are less likely to get divorced, older people are *more* likely to get divorced. They say, "The same people who had unprecedented divorce incidence in 1980 and 1990 when they were in their 20s and 30s are now in their 40s, 50s, and 60s. The Baby Boom generation was responsible for the extraordinary rise in marital instability after 1970. They are now middle-aged, but their pattern of high marital instability continues."[10]

It turns out boomers are not going to "settle down" when they age. The incessant barrage of commercials for Viagra and Cialis shows adults in their fifties and sixties as part of a new sexual revolution that uses pills to overcome the effects of aging. Online dating sites like eHarmony, match.com, and OurTime.com are not just for the young.

Dr. Susan Brown, who has studied the graying of divorce, is concerned about the economic and health issues of single boomers. For previous generations, spouses were the first line of defense for illness and long-term care. But as a growing number of people over sixty-five are single, they will face these issues alone. And if they are childless or estranged from their children, this will only make matters worse. She says, "These shifting family patterns portend new strains on existing institutional supports for the elderly. As more singles enter older adulthood, we as a society may have to reconsider how we care for frail elders. The family may no longer be a viable option for an increasing segment of older adults."[11]

Loneliness on the Rise

The result of the shifting nature of boomer relationships is loneliness. Robert Weiss, in his groundbreaking book *Loneliness: The Experience of Emotional and Social Isolation*, estimated that 25 percent of Americans regularly report suffering from loneliness.[12] He said, "Loneliness is much more often commented on by songwriters than by social scientists."[13] When considering why people were reluctant to talk about it, he found that it is "such a painful, frightening experience that people will do practically everything to avoid it."[14]

One writer who was going to a conference on loneliness was on an airplane when the woman sitting next to him asked him where he was going. After he told her he was going to a conference on loneliness, she blushed, stammered, and quietly said to him, "I'm sorry."

Many have this attitude about loneliness because they think it affects only people who are painfully shy, widowed, divorced, or unhappily single. But, in fact, people in these types of situations are more likely to feel lonesome than lonely. Loneliness is something that is much deeper than a temporary condition of being alone. Weiss says:

> Loneliness appears always to be a response to the absence of some particular type of relationship or, more accurately, a response to the absence of some particular relational provision. In many instances it is a response to the absence of the provisions of a close, indeed intimate, attachment.[15]

In other words, loneliness is the result of a breakdown of meaningful relationships. Just being with someone does not bring about a cure. For example, someone who has been married for thirty years may decide he is now living with a stranger. Somewhere along the way, he lost a connection with his spouse and now feels estranged and alone in his thoughts, feelings, and hopes for the future.

Seven Elements of Relationships

In order to understand loneliness, we must first understand what it is to have a meaningful relationship. James Flanders, writing in *Loneliness: A Sourcebook of Current Theory, Research and Therapy*, developed what he called a "Concept of Human Contact."[16] In his work, he identified seven essential features of human contact.

The first two features are (1) time for frequent interactions and (2) time for informal interactions free of pressing role demands.[17] Most of the time, we interact with people on the basis of roles. At work, we interact with the boss or the secretary or the customer. In the family, we are the parent or child or husband or wife. At church, we are the layperson or the pastor. Very few are the times when we interact with people outside of these role demands.

Relationships that have long-lasting meaning have a sense of serendipity to them, of playfulness and compassion rolled into one. This happens only through frequent interactions between people who are freed from playing a part in a scripted role of life.

While people may be aware of the need for time for these kinds of interactions, finding the time to be in deep relationships is becoming more difficult because of the increasing demands that are placed upon them. While at one time home was a sanctuary that gave people a break from the workplace, with the advent of smartphones, computers, and tablets, work is only a text or email away.

Boomers are not only strained for time in relation to husbands or wives or meaningful others; children and parents also make demands on their time. One of the most pressing concerns for boomers is how to take care of their parents who need more care and attention as they grow older. A report from the Older Women's League found that women can expect to spend seventeen years of their lives raising children and eighteen years helping an aging parent.[18]

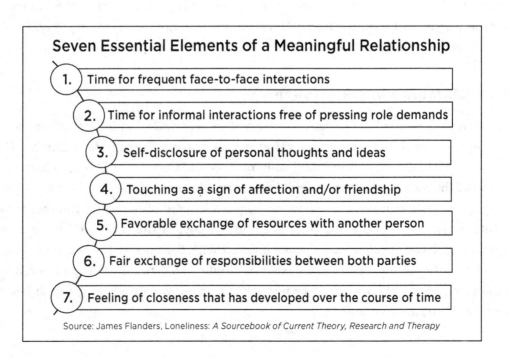

Seven Essential Elements of a Meaningful Relationship

1. Time for frequent face-to-face interactions
2. Time for informal interactions free of pressing role demands
3. Self-disclosure of personal thoughts and ideas
4. Touching as a sign of affection and/or friendship
5. Favorable exchange of resources with another person
6. Fair exchange of responsibilities between both parties
7. Feeling of closeness that has developed over the course of time

Source: James Flanders, Loneliness: *A Sourcebook of Current Theory, Research and Therapy*

More and more boomers are faced with the heartrending decision of how to take care of parents who can no longer live on their own. Should they bring parents into their own house, find a retirement home, or put them in a rest home? As boomers and their parents age, these are some of the hardest choices they will ever face.

As a result, many boomers find themselves caught in a web of demands from a variety of sources—from work to home, from children to parents to friends and relatives, and on and on it goes.

Any group that seeks the help of boomers to do its work—whether it is the church, the Red Cross, or any community organization—needs to realize that boomers are far more likely to be willing to pay to get something done than to volunteer their time. Anyone who asks boomers to come to a meeting or an activity had better make sure it is worth their time or that person will never see those boomers again. Because boomers recognize how little time they have to develop meaningful and lasting relationships, their most important commodity is time, not money.

A third feature of human contact is self-disclosure,[19] the willingness and ability to share one's deepest feelings and emotions in a safe and trustworthy environment. Self-disclosure is something that develops over the length of a relationship. Sadly for boomers, they are more likely to have to buy this type of relationship by going to a counselor than to find it in their daily interactions with people who are the close to them.

Boomers are far more likely to talk to a psychologist than to a friend, pastor, or family member about a problem they are experiencing. A number of them, at the least sign of trouble with a child, will take that child to a child psychologist to try to straighten things out. Earlier in our history, the extended family provided an environment of trust where self-disclosure could happen. In the world of the boomer, self-disclosure takes place in the office of a psychologist or in the midst of a circle of strangers.

The Loneliness of Boomer Men

While the familiar image of loneliness is an older woman sitting alone in front of a TV, the reality is that boomer men are the most vulnerable to the deadly results of loneliness—suicide. Robin Williams's suicide was not an exceptional event when seen in the wider context of his generation. Boomer men are 60 percent more likely to kill themselves than men in their parents' or grandparents' generations.

Julie Phillips, a sociology professor at Rutgers, points to three factors that have an impact on boomer men. First, boomer men who have been divorced are living alone. If they have children, most of them are estranged from them because—in most cases—the men paid child-support to the ex-wives, and the children lived with their mother.

Second, the Great Recession hit men in their fifties the hardest, especially those in blue-collar jobs or those who were phased out because they were not able to keep up with the transition to the use of digital technology in the workplace.

Third, unlike men in previous generations, old age is not moving them to become more religious. Phillips says there is no indication that as boomer men age, they will suddenly start going back to church. As a result, they do not have the benefit of a social network or belief system to help them navigate life issues such as illnesses or loss of income.

Phillips says, "We're in a position now where suicide rates for middle-aged people are higher than those for the elderly. That hasn't happened before, at least not in the last century. The concern is that as those middle-aged people move into old age, where suicide rates are typically higher for men at least, we may see them get higher still."[20]

The fourth feature of human contact is touching.[21] We live in a world that is increasingly high tech and low touch. Instead of playing ball with friends, children are more likely to play a video game in front of a TV monitor. Television, computers, and ATMs are increasingly replacing people. Louise Bernikow, writer of *Alone in America: The Search for Companionship*, says,

> American life has become privatized. People are wrapped up in selfish, individual pursuits of material goods. We're not often encouraged to value people.
>
> We also live in a world where it's not so clear what other people are for any more. . . . All the advances in our life may not cause isolation, but they have made it more possible to live that way.[22]

In our fast-paced, win-at-any-cost, individualistic society, millions of people can go weeks at a time without a hug or the touch of a loved one. Monkeys in cages at the zoo give more attention to one another than many of us humans give to one another in our daily lives. One of the saddest results of loneliness is that when people are out of contact with others, they become untouchable, not because of disease, but because they feel they do not have permission to touch other people.

The Challenge of Marriage

The fifth feature of human contact is the *favorable* exchange of resources, which must occur over months and years. This exchange has a value that cannot be found in any other way. Worth is found in the relationship itself. More important, there is something special created because the person involved is willing to give of himself or herself to the other person. He or she is willing to invest in the other what is most precious— time and attention.[23]

A century ago, marriage offered a number of resources that were in high demand, and the institution of marriage provided a favorable exchange of resources. First, there was the sexual relationship between husband and wife, in which monogamy was the ideal. Second was the economic necessity of teaming up: the husband took care of the work outside the home, and the wife took care of the children and the housework. Third, the clear-cut roles of husband and wife made it socially unacceptable to be unmarried. Society demanded marriage as a moral absolute. To be unattached was to live outside the norms of civilized society.

For boomers and younger generations, things are much different than for previous generations. Today's norms are much more permissive than norms of the past. As a result, society has made it possible to have sexual needs satisfied by a number of different partners. Men and women alike have the freedom to experiment. Society's standards have changed so rapidly that almost any kind of behavior and lifestyle seems to be acceptable as long as it is "safe."

Things have changed in the economic sphere as well. Women today are able to sustain themselves economically outside of marriage, although many boomers will tell you it takes two checks to live the American dream.

If sexual and economic needs can be met on an individual basis and if any lifestyle is acceptable, what scarce commodity do people have to offer to one another in today's world? The answer is companionship—not love, not money, not sex, not material goods, but spending quality time with a person over weeks, months, and years. For boomers, the scarce commodity they seek is not someone who will sleep with them, but someone who will stay with them even in their darkest hours.

The sixth feature of human contact that brings with it a lasting relationship is a *fair* exchange of responsibilities between both parties. More than talking about equality in relationships, this refers to how much each person is willing to invest in and to give to the other person. This is especially important in the raising of children. To maintain strong and resilient ties with a child, parents must give at considerable cost to themselves. One of the stark realities of divorce is what happens in the relationship between children of divorce and their fathers.

Suzanne M. Bianchi and Judith A. Seltzer, in an *American Demographics* article, "Life without Father," talk about what life was like for divorced boomers who had young children. "Mom and Dad are divorced. Dad drops by on Saturdays to take the kids to the zoo. This stereotypical image softens the harsh realities of divorce. But most of the children of divorced parents must live with the realities. Over half see their absent parents (nine out of ten times their father) less than once a month. One-third never see their father."[24]

When I pastored churches in the 1990s, I came into contact with these children all the time. I called them the "shuttle kids" because they were moved from parent to parent on different weekends and holidays, depending on whose turn it was to have them. Many times, I got the impression that the parent who got them had won the booby prize for that weekend. The effect on children in these situations was damaging to their sense of identity. Although they appeared to be thick-skinned survivors who could take on the world, many of them in private confessed to a deep longing for continuity and lasting love. Many admitted to feeling very lonely.

Now that these children are grown, many have put off getting married and having children. Those who have families try not to follow their parents' example. And in many cases, the children who felt the effect of their parents' separation when they were young want very little to do with their parents now.

The question for boomers as they live in the second half of life is this: As they age, who is going to take care of the fathers and mothers who failed to see their children when they were young? Who will be the caregivers to the millions of single elderly who have become estranged from their children as a result of divorce and separation? Why would the children of boomers who felt abandoned when they were young want to help their parents when their parents are old?

Cheryl Russell wrote in *100 Predictions for the Baby Boom* that the decisions boomers made when they were younger now affect their lives as they age. The happiness of boomers in their old age hinges on two things, "children and money." Of children, she says,

> Unfortunately, most Americans believe the myth that parents cannot count on their children in old age. Because American society has been so slow to adjust to the new rules of economic life, it is doubly hard for the baby boom to make the best long-term investment that it can make—the investment in children.[25]

Because boomers focused on short-term rewards in the past, they failed to see the long-term results of their unwillingness to invest in relationships. If the outlook was constantly "What's in it for me?" it's hard to understand what reciprocal benefits you get from a relationship that seems to be going nowhere.

Enduring family partnerships require considerable personal cost and work. Marriages do not just happen. After the bliss of the honeymoon, there comes a time of learning to live together. Parenting is not automatic. It takes commitment and endurance to raise a child. It takes patience to wait for the long-term rewards of building lasting relationships, patience that many boomers never learned to develop.

The seventh factor in developing human contact that leads to long-lasting relationships is a feeling of closeness. Flanders says that the biggest block to developing closeness is the raising of expectations that other people are not able to fulfill.[26] One characteristic of boomers that leads to loneliness is their high expectations, which are very hard to meet. Raised in an era of economic growth and abundance, they have come to expect a lot out of life.

Susan Littwin, who told us about Kathleen, the young woman who did not want to admit that she was married, says that beyond expectations, many boomers have lived with a sense of entitlement.

Like the children of the very rich, middle-class children raised in the 1960s exhibit much of the same attitude.

> They put a great emphasis on the self, dislike answering to others, believe that things will somehow work out for the best, that their fantasies will come true, and that the world they move in will be strung with safety nets. Many add special expectations of their own to this already heady brew. Some of them feel entitled to good times, expensive equipment, and the kind of homes they grew up in. Others believe their rights include instant status, important, meaningful work, and an unspoiled environment.
>
> All of them believed that they had limitless choices, arrayed like cereals on the market shelves.[27]

Unlike their parents, who were raised in the Depression years and learned to sacrifice and save for the future, boomers want instant gratification.

As boomers face the problem of unfulfilled expectations in their economic lives, even more unsettling are their unmet expectations in their personal lives. Raised on a steady diet of TV sitcoms in which problems were solved with a slogan and a laugh within thirty minutes, the immediacy of ongoing problems nags at what they thought life was supposed to be.

One boomer remembers being told how wonderful she and her classmates were by their teachers at school. "After the first moon landing, our teacher told us that we were God's children, and that the world was ours."[28] The problem with this mentality is that if you come to believe that the world is yours, it is hard to understand why your spouse would rather watch a football game than engage you in a conversation.

The Problem of "Living Together Loneliness"

As boomers struggle to find some closure in their relationships, to have a feeling of closeness with another human being, they continually fight the image of the perfect marriage, the perfect family, and the perfect lover, which no one this side of heaven will be able to live up to.

Martin E. P. Seligman in an article on "Boomer Blues" says, Married partners once settled for duty, but today's mates expect to be ecstatic lovers, intellectual colleagues and partners in tennis and water sports. We even expect our partners to be loving parents. . . . It's as if some idiot raised the ante on what it takes to be a normal human being. We blindly accept this rush of rising expectations for the self. What's remarkable is not that we fail on some but that we achieve so many.[29]

In *Living Together, Feeling Alone*, Dr. Dan Kiley has identified a type of loneliness he calls "Living Together Loneliness," a condition that has emerged in the last twenty years. He defines loneliness as "a person's emotional response to a perceived discrepancy between expected and achieved social contact."[30]

Kiley says the key word in this definition is *expected*. "Fifty years ago, most of our grandmas didn't expect their men to give them intimacy, sharing, and emotional belonging. This doesn't mean that they didn't want it or need it; they simply didn't expect it. They may have been disappointed or sad, but without the expectation for closeness, they didn't experience the very private emotion of loneliness."[31]

Spouses who are married but who feel that their partners have let them down primarily experience living together loneliness. Because loneliness is associated with being alone, they don't identify loneliness as being their problem. Instead, the problem seems to be with their husband or wife or lover who does not pay them enough attention, is always too busy to talk to them, or ignores their needs. As their loneliness increases, they go through the stages of bewilderment, isolation, agitation, depression, and finally exhaustion.[32]

Unmet expectations also affect boomers in their work. I know of one extremely successful businessman who "has it made." Everything he touches turns to gold, but he never can seem to get enough. He is estranged from his wife and children. He has all the wealth in the world. But now that he has made it, he asks, "Is that all there is?"

A highly successful accountant gave me this analogy to his life. He said that his career has been like scaling a cliff. When he graduated from college, he and his friends and family started together at the bottom of the cliff, taking the first steps up together.

When they got to a rough spot, he would reach over to help them up. As he got higher and higher, the cliff got more treacherous and narrow. So instead of reaching down to help others, he found himself scratching and clawing his way over the backs of those ahead of him. Finally, after years of struggle and fighting his way up, he made it to the top only to find himself all alone. As he looked over the edge of the cliff, he could see his wife, children, and friends dashed against the rocks at the bottom of the cliff. He had made it to the top, but it had cost him all the people he had loved. Now he wonders if there is any more to life.

As boomers are caught in the trap of rising personal expectations that never seem to be met, they find themselves in a state of emotional isolation. Cut off from meaningful and lasting relationships, millions of boomers are what they never expected to be—lonely. Kiley says this problem is fundamentally a spiritual problem.

> Because a lonely feeling is such a subjective experience, and almost never replicates itself, it's impossible to measure loneliness objectively. Consequently, the treatment program must involve some degree of spirituality; that is, asking a person to search for greater meaning in his or her life.[33]

Instead of searching for greater spiritual meaning in life, most lonely people find themselves trying to escape from their feelings and thus live a lifestyle that is characterized by rootlessness. What Weiss identifies as social isolation,[34] boomers experience as a constant search for something that will make them happy, something that will give them a lift, something that will make them feel satisfied.

As if that is not enough, as boomers live the second half of life, they face a rapidly changing world where the old rules of politics, economics, and morality do not work any more. While they grew up with the mantra of "you will make a difference in this world," the reality is today's world is much different from what anyone expected. It's to that constantly changing world and its resulting loss of stability we now turn.

CHAPTER
3

Rootlessness

In the summer of 1973 I was one of more than 800,000 U.S. boomers who traveled to Europe. Unlike most who went traveling on their own, I went the safe way, on a tour with a Latin club. I remember the comical scene in the airport when it dawned on me that I was to spend my six-week discovery trip with about thirty-four retired Latin teachers and seven fellow boomers. I think my parents were relieved to see what good supervision I would be under, as this was my first major trip away from home. It was also good for my biceps, as I spent much of the time carrying bags for a group of retired teachers who were ready to live it up.

One scene from that trip stands out in my mind. We were riding in a tour bus past the center of Amsterdam when the tour guide pointed out "Hippie Square," where hundreds of hippies dressed in the garb of flower children were sitting and smoking marijuana. Raised in a conservative home, I had never seen a group of real hippies, except at the Tournament of Roses Parade, but that was no big deal, because everyone acted strange on New Year's Day in Pasadena. But here in Amsterdam was a group of people from my own country who seemed to come from a far different place than I did. Far from being fellow citizens, they looked as if they had come from another planet. Yet these American youth were part of a great migration that was taking place in the late '60s and early '70s.

Annie Gottlieb in *Do You Believe in Magic?* describes the feeling of those who were on the move at that time.

> That urge for wholeness would drive us to discover and embrace everything our own culture had put down or ruled out. The children of security, we hankered for risk. Children of the "nice," the reasonable and rational, we wanted vision, passion, pain. Children of technology, we longed to get our hands in the dirt. Children of Lysol, Listerine, and Wonder Bread, we were starved for texture, taste, and smell. It was all "out there," outside those sterile space colonies, the suburbs; on the road, on the land, among people who had nothing much but life itself.[1]

The boomers I saw in Amsterdam were just the tip of the iceberg. In the late '60s and early '70s millions of boomers were dropping out of traditional American society. Sporting long hair and love beads, they became part of the movement that wanted no part of the establishment. They hitchhiked on streets and freeways. They bought a Eurail pass and traveled throughout Europe living in youth hostels. They bought Volkswagen vans and toured the world, going wherever they felt led. The one thing they did not do was to go where anyone wanted them to go; they had a mind and an agenda of their own.

Parents of boomers were very much aware of the rebellion of their children against the established rules and values of society. Midge Decter, a parent of boomers, wrote:

> As children of this peculiar enlightened class, you were expected one day to be manning a more than proportional share of the positions of power and prestige in this society: you were to be its executives, its professionals, its artists and intellectuals, among its business and political leaders, you were to think its influential thoughts, tend its major institutions, and reap its highest rewards. . . . Beneath these throbbing ambitions were all the ordinary—if you will, mundane—hopes that all parents harbor for their children: that you would grow up, come into your own, and with all due happiness and high spirit carry forward the normal human business of mating, home-building, and reproducing—replacing us, in other words, in the eternal human cycle.[2]

Boomers, who were fully aware of these unspoken expectations, thought there should be more to life than a nine-to-five job, a Buick in the garage, and a house on Elm Street. They wanted their lives to have meaning and purpose; if they could not have that, they at least wanted to enjoy life and have fun. They wanted to experience all the world had to offer; they wanted to go beyond the survivor mentality of Depression babies; they wanted to have it all.

Every belief, idea, and tradition was up for grabs. Whether it was belief in the Christian God or democracy or wearing a suit and tie to work, boomers were ready to replace it with Eastern religions, socialism, or bell-bottom jeans. The argument ran something like this: "Look at the mess you have made of the world. Nuclear arms, Vietnam, racial inequality, sexism, and pollution are destroying the world. Give us our chance. We can do better."

The end result of this rebellion against the traditions and viewpoints of the past was rootlessness, focusing on personal needs and wants without having a sense of history or traditional beliefs to give a person guidance. Boomers became disconnected from the institutions that held society together in an attempt to make a more just and loving world, but found that they had to make new rules and regulations as they went along. So change was embraced with a vengeance without the safety net of faith, community, or common culture to catch people when they fell.

Many thought this would just be a phase that boomers went through as they lived their youthful years. However, rather than abating, rootlessness persists to this day. Whereas loneliness is born out of unmet needs in personal interactions, rootlessness has as its source unmet expectations in relationship to society as a whole.

From the Start, Boomers Were Treated Differently

One may wonder how it came about that a whole generation would come to feel as though it was different from the rest, that its perspectives and values were far more insightful than the views that had been handed down from previous generations. To understand how this happened, we have to take a step back into history to see that from the start, boomers were treated much differently from generations that had come before.

Before the 1950s, children went directly from childhood into adulthood; there was no distinct period from age thirteen to age twenty-one, which we now call the teenage years. A young person left childhood gradually and went into the working world. Only the lucky and the few continued their education. Before World War II, a person with a high-school education was considered to be trained and ready to take on responsibilities in the adult world of work.

But the 1950s brought a turn of events. For the first time, blue-collar workers had enough earning power to live middle-class lives. Spurred on by postwar productivity and the expansion of the economy, unions had won great victories for their workers. In 1925, blue-collar workers in manufacturing industries had become the largest single occupational group in the United States. As a result of their numbers, the unions and the people they represented became the dominant political force in the '50s. In the economy of the 1950s and '60s, all a person needed to advance in American society into a middle-class lifestyle was a union card and a willingness to learn a skill in the manufacturing industries.[3]

As blue-collar workers lived middle-class lifestyles, they took on the values and the dreams of the middle class. In the '50s, more than half of all Americans lived what is now called a traditional lifestyle, with the father working and the mother staying home with the children. A 1959 survey found that three-quarters of all American couples wanted traditional families of three or more children.[4] Because of blue-collar gains, there was little difference between the lifestyles of the middle class and the working class. A middle-class person might have a bigger house or a deeper carpet than a blue-collar worker, but for the most part, everyone had the same type of consumer items.[5]

The newfangled goods of the '50s and early '60s were durable items such as refrigerators, washing machines, cars, and televisions. While the middle class settled into a mundane lifestyle, which even the advertising industry found safe and dull,[6] blue-collar workers began feeling as though they finally had it made. Boomers' parents were not afraid to tell their children that they had lived through a depression and a war to get what they had. It had taken them a lifetime to acquire the trappings of the American dream.

Although the earnings gap between professional or managerial workers and industrial workers had not changed much in the '50s, one of the great boasts of the time was that in the new suburbs a plumber could live next to a professor and an electrician could live next to a doctor. There was virtually no difference in lifestyle between them: all could drive the same cars and live in the same houses.[7]

In the midst of plenty and apparent affluence for all, the consumer culture was born. The innocent purchase of a television allowed an array of uninvited guests to visit the living room of the American household. For the first time, advertisers were able to penetrate into the homes of all classes of Americans throughout the country and encourage them to buy the goods that proved they had arrived. One of the groups that marketers found to be the most profitable was the babies and children who made up the baby boom. As Ken Dychtwald says in *Age Wave*:

> When the boomers arrived, the diaper industry prospered. When they took their first steps, the shoe and photo industries skyrocketed. The baby-food industry, which had moved 270 million jars in 1940, ladled out enough strained meals to fill 1.5 billion jars a year by 1953. The boom kids created an insatiable demand for the sugarcoated cereals and toys hyped on Saturday-morning cartoon shows. Cowboy outfits, very popular with toddlers in the 1950s, rang up sales of $75 million per year. As the boomers suffered scraped knees and runny noses, a massive pediatric medical establishment arose, and Dr. Spock became a national figure.[8]

While boomers spent the 1950s as children (a baby born in 1946 would be thirteen years old in 1959), their older siblings, cousins, and acquaintances created the first teen culture. Known as the pioneers and the silent generation, the generation that preceded the boomers was the first group of adolescents to become a market to whom goods could be sold. Teen clothes, teen movies, teen music, and teen fads became the rage. Although class and race divided American teenagers, marketing firms did their best to promote a universal teen identity.

As American adults labored for dull durable products, teenagers of the 1950s bought goods that were exciting and flashy. With the focus on their needs and wants, companies fell all over themselves to supply teens with their every need and desire—for a good reason: it was immensely profitable. By 1955 teenagers were purchasing 43 percent of all records, 44 percent of all cameras, 39 percent of all radios, 9 percent of all new cars, and an unbelievable 53 percent of all movie tickets. By 1959, the amount of money spent on teenagers by themselves and by their parents had reached a staggering total of $10 billion a year.[9]

The 60s Vanguard Set the Trends for the Younger Boomers

The leaders of the youth culture came from an unexpected source—from the American lower class and from working-class England. Elvis Presley, the Beatles, the Doors, the Rolling Stones, the Supremes, and Bob Dylan were not the kids you would meet down the block in a nice middle-class neighborhood. They also were not boomers. Born during WWII, from 1934–1945, they became the voices of the sixties revolution.

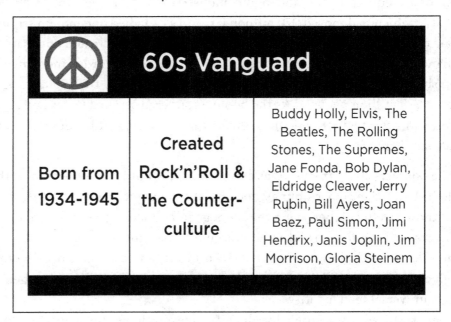

	60s Vanguard	
Born from 1934-1945	Created Rock'n'Roll & the Counter-culture	Buddy Holly, Elvis, The Beatles, The Rolling Stones, The Supremes, Jane Fonda, Bob Dylan, Eldridge Cleaver, Jerry Rubin, Bill Ayers, Joan Baez, Paul Simon, Jimi Hendrix, Janis Joplin, Jim Morrison, Gloria Steinem

Far from having the boyish charm of Wally in *Leave It to Beaver*, the rock stars who became the trendsetters for the young were more apt to spring from the nightmares of parents who held middle-class values so dear. For beyond the homogenized picture of America portrayed on television was the flip side of American culture heard on the radio. Charles Kaiser in *1968 in America* says:

> TV was a white medium, the one you turned on in your living room to watch *Leave It to Beaver* or *Father Knows Best*, family entertainment that reinforced the middle-class ideal of the white suburban family. With the mass production of transistors in the late fifties, radio became the medium you could enjoy anywhere, alone, outdoors, or under the covers (even after you were supposed to be asleep). What you heard put you squarely inside a world of your own, a world just as subversive as the Frank Sinatra generation feared it might be—the raucous, untamed, black and white world of Little Richard, Elvis Presley, Jerry Lee Lewis, Buddy Holly, the jitterbug, and Murray the K.[10]

The message of rock 'n' roll had little to do with discipline, achievement, and professional careers. It was more apt to put down academics ("Another Brick in the Wall," Pink Floyd), to belittle the rigors of hard work ("Working in the Coal Mine," Lee Dorsey), or to mock authority ("Whoopee, We're All Going to Die," Country Joe and the Fish at Woodstock).

By 1965, a form of music that had been concerned with love and dancing began to convey three unmistakable messages. The first message was anger and hopelessness as seen in P. F. Sloan's "Eve of Destruction." Released in August 1965, it reached the top of the charts in five weeks and was labeled the fastest-rising song in rock history. Unlike songs by the Beatles, whose songs rose on the charts because of the group's popularity, "Eve of Destruction" became popular because of its message.

Its frightening words were accompanied by a pounding drumbeat that signaled that the end was near. In the decade-long history of rock 'n' roll, this song was the first to dredge up the fears of the boomer generation. Not only did it challenge the assumptions of the war in Vietnam, but it also invoked images of a coming nuclear apocalypse with words evoking the horrible scene of a world turned into a graveyard.

This was the first of a number of songs that would pound home the truth that the young lived in a precarious world that could be blown up at any minute and in which they could lose their life at the whim and mercy of those in the "establishment." After all, it was their parents' generation that invented the bomb and put them at risk. It was their parents' generation that got them into war and asked them to defend their way of life, a way of life that young people were not so sure they wanted to live.

The second message that echoed the growing discontent of the '60s came from another 1965 number one hit, the Rolling Stones' defiant "Satisfaction." The verses, which were a parody of the banality of radio, TV, and advertising, were far outshone by the chorus, which boldly proclaimed to anyone who was listening that no one was going to stop this generation from getting whatever it wanted. In *The Sixties*, Todd Gitlin noted, " 'Satisfaction' was a cross-yelp of resentment that could appeal to waitresses and mechanics and students, all stomping in unison."[11]

Beyond the themes of hopelessness and unfulfilled desires was a third theme: the hope of transcendence as exemplified by another 1965 hit, Bob Dylan's "Mr. Tambourine Man." Dylan, who had written "Blowing in the Wind," an antiwar anthem, offered to the youth of America an escape from the harsh realities of life into a transcendent state of peace and love.[12] The layered lyrics of this song moved a person into a different state of consciousness. Hearing it was not enough. What many desired was a total experience that captivated the soul and moved them to a different plane.

The Emergence of the Drug Culture

Many tried to enhance this experience with drugs. Todd Gitlin, who was part of the movement at the time, reflects that "Mr. Tambourine Man" went down especially well with marijuana, just then making its way into dissident campus circles. "People began to hear that in order to understand this and other songs, one had to smoke marijuana. Many believed that to be part of the youth culture, they had to get high. Lyrics became more elaborate, compressed, and obscure, images more gnarled, the total effect nonlinear, translinear. Without grass, you were an outsider looking in."[13]

Many early experimenters saw drugs as a way to find themselves and to see beyond the boundaries of the physical self. Like ancient mystics from the East or Native Americans sharing a peace pipe, they made it a ritual of communion with the universe.

Wynston Jones, a screenwriter says, "Drugs and the Sixties increased my tolerance for ambiguity; there is no one reality."[14] When Paul McCartney tried marijuana for the first time during a gathering between the Beatles and Dylan, he was heard to say, "I'm thinking for the first time, really thinking."[15]

LSD was taken because it was considered to be mind-expanding. Some took it as a religious rite. In Gottlieb's book, Cherel Ito says, "The friend who gave it to me dressed me in white and sat me down in front of Buddha and read me the *Tibetan Book of the Dead*. I was at Filmore East."

Another person remembers that "somebody just came up to me and said, 'Are you searching?' I said, 'Yeah.' He said, 'Here's something to help you.' And he put it in my mouth. I kept it in there, and I was very happy I did. Because it gave me the vision and the courage to actually go after what I had been longing for my whole life, and that was a spiritual quest."[16]

This ideal of LSD as a wonder drug that would help America move into a new age of freedom and love had become the grounding for the counterculture movement as exemplified in the Haight-Ashbury district in San Francisco. On January 12, 1967, Allen Cohen held a press conference in which he announced there was going to be a Human Be-In in San Francisco. Boldly, he announced:

> Now in the evolving generation of America's young the humanization of the American man and woman can begin in joy and embrace without fear, dogma, suspicion, or dialectical righteousness. A new concert of human relations being developed within the youthful underground must emerge, become conscious, and be shared so that a revolution of form can be filled with a Renaissance of compassion, awareness and love in the Revelation of the unity of all mankind.[17]

As the "be-in" started on January 14, Stanley Owsley, the pioneer of LSD production techniques whom the *Los Angeles Times* recognized as the "LSD millionaire," handed out free samples of his newest LSD product, White Lightning. A few months earlier on October 6, 1966, possessing LSD had become a misdemeanor, and selling it became a felony in California.[18] Now that it was illegal, it was even more of a turn-on. The "be-in" turned out to be the biggest acid party ever held and, in the eyes of its promoters, it was a grand success.

More than 20,000 people participated, and the news media saw it as evidence of an unexplained, unforeseen mass movement. More than anything, its mysteriousness was what attracted attention. It had Hindu, Buddhist, and Native American trappings. An astrologer had picked the date of the event. Even the Hell's Angels had played a part by volunteering to protect the sound equipment.[19]

To experts it was a confounding puzzle of drugs, politics, Eastern mysticism, and culture, which was in complete opposition to the values of traditional American society. The predominant question of the time was, "Why?" Why would these youth, who had been given all the opportunities that a modern, educated, and affluent society had to offer, want to follow Timothy Leary's slogans of "Tune in, turn on, drop out" and "Get out of your mind and into your senses"?[20] Driven by a curious mixture of fear and wonder, the news media did their best to cover the new hippie culture. Gitlin states:

Thanks to modern mass media, and to drugs—perhaps the most potent form of mass communication—notions which had been the currency of tiny groups were percolating through the vast demographics of the baby boom. *Life, Time,* and the trendspotters of the evening news outdid themselves trumpeting the new youth culture. As with the beats, cultural panic spread the news, the image of hippiehood. . . . There was enormous anxiety about whether the prevailing culture could hold the young; and on the liberal side, anxiety about whether it deserved to. It became easy to imagine that the whole of youth was regressing, or evolving, into—what? Barbarism? A new society into itself, a Woodstock Nation? A children's crusade? A subversive army? A revolutionary class? Astonishingly soon, Governor George Wallace and Dr. Timothy Leary agreed that what was at stake was nothing less than Western Civilization, the only question being whether its demise was auspicious.[21]

The Beatles added to the growing controversy about the direction the youth culture was going when the group graduated from marijuana to LSD and started writing music while high. During a tripped out session, Ringo Starr composed "Yellow Submarine."[22]

When the Beatles released the album *Sergeant Pepper's Lonely Hearts Club Band* in 1967, the oldest of the first-wave boomers were twenty-one. They were either in college, in Vietnam, or in jobs fit for high school graduates. Critics immediately hailed the Beatles' album as the best ever. Others criticized it for its alleged references to drugs. "A Day in My Life" was banned in England because Paul McCartney's lyric sounded as though he was getting high. Other songs got an equally negative review.

The song that generated the most controversy was "Lucy in the Sky with Diamonds," which sounded like something penned during an acid trip. People immediately thought that "Lucy in the Sky with Diamonds" was a anagram for LSD, but John Lennon contended it was only an accident and that this phrase was one his mother had used to describe a drawing of her he had made in school one day.[23] Peter Brown, who was the executive director of the Beatles' management company, says,

> Sergeant Pepper became . . . the album that most perfectly personified the incense-laden, rainbow-colored, psychedelic sixties themselves. With Sergeant Pepper, the Beatles ascended from pop heroes to avatars and prophets. The album was praised and dissected and studied like the Torah or the Koran.[24]

As the Beatles went, so did a whole generation. More than 50 percent, or some 35.5 million boomers say at some time in their lives they used illegal drugs. In 2015, 75 percent of boomers admitted to drug rehabilitation centers say they started using drugs before they were twenty-five.[25]

It is doubtful that any other product had as much market penetration as marijuana and LSD did in the 1960s. Like the music, these drugs cut across all class lines, from the student in college to the construction worker on the job to the soldier in Vietnam.

This desire for drugs has not abated over time. In fact, now that boomers are in their fifties and sixties, illicit drug use in these age groups has doubled. With the legalization of marijuana in states like Colorado and Washington, drug use will be sure to grow.

Aging Boomers Still Do Drugs

When boomers were in high school, the highest use of drugs of any generation was recorded in 1979. When they reached the ages of forty-nine to sixty-seven in 2013, it was estimated that over 6 percent of boomers regularly used illicit drugs, with painkillers, heroin, and cocaine being the drugs of choice. It is estimated that one in twenty boomers will need drug rehabilitation by 2020.

In 2013, the Centers for Disease Control and Prevention reported that 12,000 boomers had died of accidental overdoses. This is more than the number who had died from car accidents or influenza. For the first time, people in their fifties and sixties had a higher rate of accidental overdose than did people ages twenty-four through forty-four.[26] Jamie Huysman, clinical adviser to the senior program at Caron Treatment Center that just broke ground on a $10 million medical center in Pennsylvania that caters to older adults, said, "If you have a trigger, and your youth is caught up in that Woodstock mentality, you're going to revert back. We were pretty conditioned that we could be rebellious, that we could take drugs, and so this is how we respond today."[27]

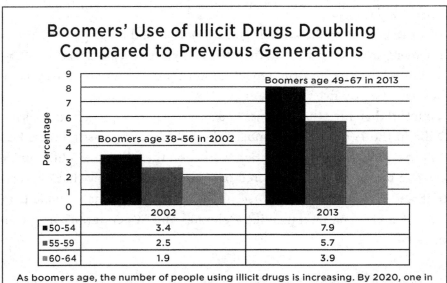

Boomers' Use of Illicit Drugs Doubling Compared to Previous Generations

Boomers age 49–67 in 2013

Boomers age 38–56 in 2002

	2002	2013
■ 50-54	3.4	7.9
■ 55-59	2.5	5.7
■ 60-64	1.9	3.9

As boomers age, the number of people using illicit drugs is increasing. By 2020, one in every 20 boomers will need drug rehabilitation, greatly exceeding previous generations.

Source: http://www.promises.com/articles/addiction/drug-use-surges-among-baby-boomers/

A *Wall Street Journal* article on the topic of drug abuse among older adults interviewed a number of boomers about their use of drugs. One Southern California executive told the story of his drug use. While in his twenties he used drugs quite often, even meth. But in his thirties, his career took off, he got married, moved to the suburbs, and had two children. And most important, he stopped using drugs.

But then in his fifties, he hurt his knee. A friend gave him a few Vicodin pills, and he was hooked. After knee surgery and an injured arm, he had a steady supply of painkillers from his doctors. After a couple of years, he would down forty a day. He was also drinking heavily. Then one day his body had enough. He had a seizure. His family had to call the paramedics to save his life. Of his experience, the man said, "What I suspect is, we [boomers] know how to get high; we know the sensation. In a broad sense, once you've been there, it's easier to get back into it."[28]

Health-care officials are concerned because rehabilitation centers and the medical establishment are not prepared for this increase of older adults who are misusing drugs. Rather than seeing a decline as this generation ages, they are anticipating a rise in the need of treatments and preventive measures as boomers age.

Beyond drugs, what united the boomer generation as none other before or since was the music and its message. To find out what boomers were thinking or believing, you had only to turn on the radio. When I gathered with my friends, it was not unusual for us to sing songs accompanied by a guitar. "Where Have All the Flowers Gone?" and "If I Had a Hammer" were songs that expressed our heart language about life. Our source of spirituality was found in the music, *our* music, not in the Bible or the beliefs of the adult society. Terri Hemmert, a boomer disk jockey in Chicago, talks about what it was like at the time.

Rock was something universal, something you understood. If you went to California to visit relatives, the kids in California knew the same songs. Your parents didn't. Maybe it was something tribal—but it was real exciting stuff.[29]

The Counterculture Loses Its Way

But by the early 1970s, something went wrong with the pop culture of the youth. The Vietnam War was grinding to an end; the counterculture was losing its impetus; the student movement was losing its cause; and the results of the high life were coming in. After the crowning achievement of mass psychedelic gatherings took place at Woodstock on August 15, 1969, the end of the movement began on December 6, 1969, at the Altamont Raceway near San Francisco at a Rolling Stones concert.

Charles Perry says of the event, "In its way, it was the topper of all the giant rock festivals, because it was the end of the series. The nasty atmosphere of panic and hostility near the stage made it the symbolic dead end of a generation's adventure. At the concert a black man, Meredith Hunter, was killed and countless others severely beaten."[30]

By this time Haight-Ashbury had moved from pot and LSD to speed, hash, heroin, and cocaine. Instead of a place of idealism, it had degenerated into a cesspool of greed, violence, and paranoia. In the first seven months of 1970, there were fourteen drug-induced murders.[31]

In the fall of 1970, Jimi Hendrix and Janis Joplin died of drug overdoses. A few months later, Jim Morrison collapsed and died, perhaps of drugs. All three were twenty-seven. In the same year, the Beatles broke up, and in 1971 John Lennon proclaimed, "The Dream Is Over."[32]

The vision promoted by the 1960s vanguard of the previous generation and first-wave boomers divided all boomers into two competing branches, the liberals and the conservatives. While the counterculture movement was squarely in the liberal camp, those who did not buy in to the values of the "drop in, drop out" culture embraced the conservative movement.

As the election of 1972 neared, many thought George McGovern would greatly benefit from the support of a new group of voters, those age eighteen to twenty. In 1971, the Twenty-sixth Amendment was added to the U.S. Constitution, which lowered the voting age to eighteen and above. Supporters of lowering the voting age won the argument when they pointed out that if you are old enough to go and die in Vietnam, you should be old enough to vote. So in 1972, boomers born from 1952 to 1954 were the first eighteen to twenty-year-olds to vote in a national election.

To the surprise of many, the majority of boomers chose Richard Nixon over McGovern. One commentator of the time said, "The simpleminded extrapolation is that youth is radical and therefore it will vote very liberal or radical. Well, somebody forgot all about Western Illinois University and Washington State and Pepperdine. Radical students are a very small slice of the action."[33]

The reelection of Richard Nixon in 1972 was largely credited to his ability to connect with the silent majority by taking on "radicals" as exemplified by the Chicago 7, who were tried for their protests during the 1968 Democratic Convention; the Weather Underground, who took part in a number of bombings in what today we would call domestic terrorism; and the Black Panther Party, whose protests against police brutality led to a national movement of liberation for blacks.

The 70s Belonged to the Second-Wave and Third-Wave Boomers

While the sixties belonged to first-wave boomers, the seventies was the decade in which the second- and third-wave boomers went through high school and college. In 1972, rock 'n' roll gave way to pop music, with The Jackson Five, David Cassidy, the Carpenters, and the Osmond Brothers taking over the top of the charts. Teenyboppers supplanted hippies, as the youth culture veered away from the excesses of the '60s music scene. Parents took a collective gasp for breath, hoping that wholesomeness would bring some measure of sanity to the teenage scene.

Later in the decade, *Saturday Night Fever* staring John Travolta and the soundtrack of the Bee Gees drew back the curtain on the grittiness of the lives of urban young adult boomers and fueled an explosion of disco music. Donna Summer became the queen of disco with her hits "Last Dance" and "On the Radio." Leisure suits replaced love beads, and platform shoes replaced leather sandals.

In the larger picture, the 1970s was a decade of decline for American influence. In 1973, the United States stopped direct military involvement in Vietnam; and in 1975, the world was greeted with pictures of South Vietnamese refugees fleeing their country after the fall of Saigon.

In 1974 Nixon was impeached, and he resigned from the presidency. In 1979, the Iran Hostage Crisis captured American's attention. Ted Koppel did his nightly count-down on ABC's *Nightline*, noting 444 days of captivity for the hostages in Iran.

The Yuppies and the Would-Be's

But what hit boomers the hardest was the economic decline that started with the recession of 1973 and the quadrupling of oil prices after an embargo by OPEC in protest of the United States' support of Israel.

Because of the sheer size of their generation, boomers entered the workforce at a disadvantage. They were the most educated generation America had ever seen. Eighty-five percent finished high school, 50 percent attended college, 25 percent graduated, and 7 percent went on to graduate school. This compares to their parents' generation, of whom 50 percent were high school graduates and 10 percent finished college.

When they graduated from college, many got a rude shock. From 1969 to 1976, eight million college graduates entered the workforce, which was twice the number of the preceding seven years. Twenty-seven percent, or 2.1 million, were forced to take jobs they had not been trained for—or were unable to find work at all.[34]

Many of those who found themselves not welcome in the workforce were those who were the most idealistic. Instead of concentrating on science, business, or engineering, they had studied social science, history, or romance languages in college, which were at the heart of a liberal arts major. Many of these same people went into the helping professions, such as teaching, social work, church work, and nursing. As much as they wanted to help others, their pay was low.

By the 1980s, the idealism of many college-educated boomers was tempered by a more urgent need—getting a job. Samantha Harrison, who during this time went back to college to get a master's in business, said, "The last two taxi drivers I had were Ph.D.'s in liberal arts." Talking about her friends, she said:

More and more young women are abandoning teaching, social work, nursing, for business. That's where the money is. . . . The people I hang out with are all over thirty. With liberal arts backgrounds. We talk about what we're gonna do when we grow up, when we get out of business school. It's a change of life in a way, being here. We've formed a Renaissance Club, yakkin' about Shakespeare, theater, books, politics. We don't want to become these little number crunching automatons.[35]

Harrison and her friends were what Peter Kim, the former senior vice president for research at J. Walter Thompson, called "would be's." They constituted the largest portion of the educated boomers who, in spite of their education, found themselves with low incomes. They were heavy into contemporary lifestyles and tended to be liberal. They were called "would-be's" because they were the part of the middle class who experienced downward mobility. As a result, they were the poor cousins of the yuppies.

Yuppies, who became the proverbial image of boomers in the mid-1980s, tended to be younger boomers who hit it big in the business world. Yuppies were found in professional and managerial positions and were seen as the leading trendsetters for their generation. They were the ones who embraced bringing their children into the world as they put "Baby On Board" signs in their Volvos. They were the people featured in TV shows such as *L.A. Law*. Tough, aggressive, and highly successful in their careers, they were the ones former '60s activists said had sold out to the establishment.[36]

Katy Butler talked of her feelings about herself in relation to the successful portrait of the yuppies: "Meanwhile, the newspapers were full of stories about yuppies and blackened redfish and new restaurants. The cognitive dissonance hurt my head: Was I the only one who felt like a failure? Was it only my friends who were in trouble?"[37]

This feeling of failure, of not making it, is the one thing that hurt would-be's the most. Caught between the altruistic beliefs of helping others and the economic necessity of making a living, they found themselves going back to school to be retrained, or changing jobs in rapid succession, or just giving up.

But even the yuppies found themselves in an unsettled position. After the stock market crash on Black Monday, October 19, 1987, Jack Maurer, who made his living on

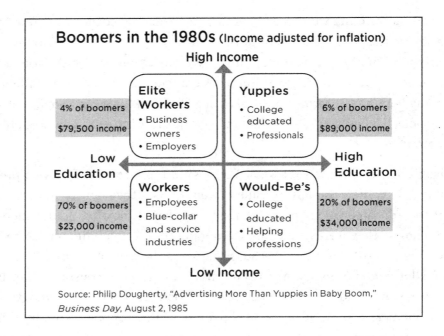

Boomers in the 1980s (Income adjusted for inflation)

High Income

Elite Workers
- Business owners
- Employers

4% of boomers

$79,500 income

Yuppies
- College educated
- Professionals

6% of boomers

$89,000 income

Low Education | High Education

Workers
- Employees
- Blue-collar and service industries

70% of boomers

$23,000 income

Would-Be's
- College educated
- Helping professions

20% of boomers

$34,000 income

Low Income

Source: Philip Dougherty, "Advertising More Than Yuppies in Baby Boom," *Business Day*, August 2, 1985

the Chicago Board of Trade, talked about the results of the crash to his fellow workers, most of whom were yuppies.

> Hey what's this gonna lead to? Lunchtime conversations have changed. They wonder about a cyclical depression. They wonder about their lifestyles. There's a lesson, important to all of us: it can happen. It means being born in the forties and fifties doesn't mean being born in an amusement park, where things are always wonderful. Generally, this is the way these white middle-class kids feel. In one day, they've discovered the world is a serious, potentially disruptive place. Nobody owes them a living. Nobody owes them luxury and good times. . . . They are beginning to realize the all-day joyride may be over.[38]

Walter Shapiro, in a 1991 article in *Time* called "The Birth and—Maybe—Death of Yuppiedom," gave a postmortem to the term that started in 1983 as a successor to *preppie* and summed up the fast-track living of boomers in the '80s. In the '90s, it lost its validity because yuppies were souring on materialism and were looking for something else. But he warned not to give up on them too fast, for although the term may have lost its glitter, there is still the taste of the good life on the lips of boomers who experienced it in the '80s.[39]

But yuppies, who received most of the spotlight, made up only 6 percent of the boomer population. They were outnumbered by would-be's, who made up 20 percent of this generation. Two other economic groups, the elite workers (4%) and workers (70%) rounded out the economic profile of the generation. Elite workers were skilled workers who did not go to college or finish their college education but who had yuppie incomes because they owned their own businesses. They were what Peter Kim called "the silent majority of the affluent market."[40]

The largest group of boomers was workers.[41] Largely ignored in the public eye, they were the ones who suffered the most from the loss of blue-collar jobs. Unlike their fathers who were in secure union jobs or who made a good living on the farm, they faced an uncertain future. Since a high point in the 1970s, the working class has

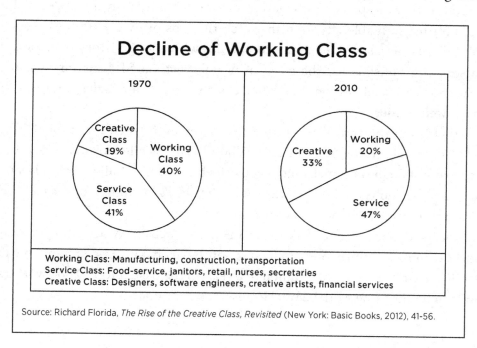

Decline of Working Class

1970

Creative Class 19%

Working Class 40%

Service Class 41%

2010

Working 20%

Creative 33%

Service 47%

Working Class: Manufacturing, construction, transportation
Service Class: Food-service, janitors, retail, nurses, secretaries
Creative Class: Designers, software engineers, creative artists, financial services

Source: Richard Florida, *The Rise of the Creative Class, Revisited* (New York: Basic Books, 2012), 41-56.

declined from 40 percent of the workforce to 20 percent. These well-paying union jobs with pensions and health care provided workers with a middle-class income.

Now that those jobs are gone, these same people moved into lower-paying service-sector jobs in retail and food service, and most do not have the same benefits. Many older workers in their fifties and sixties have quit the job force completely by getting by on their spouse's income or moving from one part-time job to another.[42]

The Parable of the Hostess Twinkie

To understand what has happened to the American worker, just look at the story of the Hostess Twinkie, a mainstay of boomer lunchboxes when boomers were children. In 2012, headlines around the country announced that Hostess had declared bankruptcy. Suddenly, people who had not had Twinkies in years were grabbing them off store shelves and selling them on eBay before they were gone forever.

What happened? A combination of a change in consumer habits, mismanagement, and a looming pension obligation of over $2 billion in unfunded liabilities created an unsustainable situation in which the jobs of over 19,000 workers at 36 different plants were lost. Like many companies with a long history of labor unions, Hostess was responsible for the costs of heavily negotiated deals for pension and medical care with their unions. As labor costs escalated and sales diminished, the company went under.[43]

But that is not the end of the story. In 2015 *Forbes* featured a story on "Twinkie's Miracle Comeback: Inside Story of a $2 Billion Feast." While Hostess ceased to exist as a company, it did have something of value, its brand. Enter billionaire C. Dean Metropoulos and Apollo Global's Andy Jhawar, who paid $410 million for the cake brands and invested another $250 million to restart the business.

Two years after bankruptcy, Twinkies made a comeback. A new 500-person plant in Kansas complete with robotics and a state-of-the-art baking system now churns out one million Twinkies a day, 400 million in a year. In the past, it took 9,000 workers and 14 plants to do the same work before Hostess closed its doors.[44]

The Great Recession Hits Boomers Hard

As working class jobs have been sent offshore and robots have replaced people, the jobs that served as the backbone of the middle class for the parents of boomers have been cut in half. The Great Recession of 2008, which led to the shedding of millions of jobs, hit boomer men in their fifties especially hard. Beyond losing jobs, millions lost their homes to foreclosure or had to withdraw funds from their 401(k) plans to make ends meet. Rather than saving for retirement, any income these boomers had went toward surviving to the next day.

Beyond the troubles of the working class, what hit boomers the hardest was the lost decade of housing values of the 2000s. After the stock market crash of 2001, Nasdaq had lost 72 percent of its value and the Dow Jones had lost 30 percent of its value.[45] People were looking for safe places to put their money, so they poured their money into their homes.

From 2000 to 2006, the national home price index increased from $108,000 to $183,000, which was over a 50 percent increase in value.[46] Even if people kept their homes, aggressive mortgage companies encouraged people to use the increasing values of their homes like an ATM machine. Need to finance your child's college education? Need to pay off credit card debt? Want to add that new sunroom? Just refinance. Don't worry, when you sell your home, you will get it all back and still make a profit.

From 2001 to 2007, the total amount of mortgage debt went from $7.5 billion to $14.6 billion.[47] Millions of homeowners hoping to cash in on the rising values of their homes refinanced and used their new-found wealth for room additions, vacations, college educations for the children, and care for aging parents.

TV shows such as *Flip This House* encouraged people to sell their homes and to move to bigger homes. While the average square feet of a house in 1980 was 1,760, by 2007 it topped out at 2,521.[48] Soon McMansions were being built in retirement havens like Phoenix, Las Vegas, and Orlando.

In the outer suburbs of Los Angeles, waves of homes were going up to attract first-time Gen X buyers and boomers who wanted to move up to larger homes. First-wave boomers were selling homes in Los Angeles and New York and taking their money with them. Many figured they could start a new job or become a consultant or use access to the Internet to keep working. Or just retire early and do part-time work.

But all that came tumbling down when the Great Recession hit the housing market. Homes that had been purchased for $400,000 were worth $150,000, and a new term was bandied about: "underwater." It meant that the value of your house was worth less than the size of your loan.

Tracts of half-built homes were abandoned as homebuilders went out of business. The number of people who had problems keeping up with their housing payments went from 4.6 percent in 2006 to 9.3 percent in 2010. The number of foreclosures went from 700,000 in 2006 to more than 2,300,000 in 2008 and 2,800,000 in 2010. More than 11,500,000 people lost their homes from 2008 to 2012.[49]

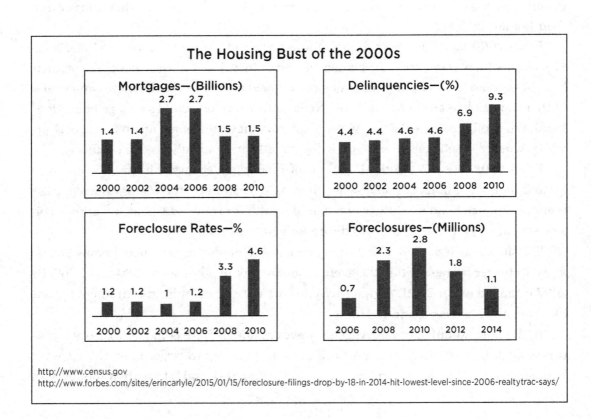

http://www.census.gov
http://www.forbes.com/sites/erincarlyle/2015/01/15/foreclosure-filings-drop-by-18-in-2014-hit-lowest-level-since-2006-realtytrac-says/

Even those who didn't lose their homes were caught in the financial fallout. City workers were called to clean out the pools from abandoned homes to cut down on the number of mosquitoes. Detroit went into bankruptcy and is in the process of tearing down more than 40,000 vacated homes.[50]

For a large portion of boomers, the 2000s were a lost decade of financial growth that kept many of them from preparing for the future. Now that a new housing boom has emerged and the stock market has recovered, boomers may feel a little safer. But those who are investing in those big homes in the suburbs might want to reconsider. *Forbes* magazine in an article on "The Great Baby Boomer Housing Bust" focuses not on the past but on the future. For if the Great Recession hit boomers hard, the generations behind them were hit even worse. In the article, author Mary Meehan says,

> We all know how the economic landscape changed in 2008. In large measure, leading up to that shift [the Great Recession], Boomers didn't save enough for retirement. For most of them, their home is their biggest asset. But many will need to sell their homes to finance their imminent post-work years. Most Boomers will want to, or need to, sell the big family homes they purchased years ago. And here's the rub: There aren't enough buyers to soak up the kind of housing inventory that downsizing Boomers will leave in their wake.[51]

Her words are something boomers definitely do not want to hear. But what she says has a lot of validity. Gen Xers and millennials do not have the capital or the income to buy the number of homes that boomers will want to sell in the future. This isn't something that will become apparent in the near-future, but by the time boomers are fully into their retirement years in the mid-2020s, many will find it very hard to sell their homes, especially if they are the big box houses that many seem to believe will ensure their financial futures.

Boomers Not Ready for Retirement

Perhaps most troubling for prognosticators is that boomers in the second half of life are ill-prepared for their retirement years. Those born just before the boomers—the 1960s vanguard—have, for the most part, gone into retirement with a combination of Social Security payments and a monthly check from their traditional pension plan (in which their employers paid for their pensions with a promise of a set payout depending on the number of years they worked).

But in 1984, a new financial instrument was created called the 401(k). It was designed to take the responsibility for retirement saving away from the employer and give it to the employee. Traditionally, a company would give a set amount toward a pension or match the employee's contribution. Called a defined benefit (DB) pension plan, it guaranteed long-term workers a set monthly income until they died. But the new pension plan, called a defined contribution (DC) plan, depended on the employee designating a set amount of his or her salary for retirement. Instead of guaranteeing a set payout like an annuity, the amount a person would receive in retirement was dependent on the stock and bond markets.

Now that boomers are in the second half of life, they are living with the decisions they made earlier in their lives. The grand experiment of employees deciding how much to put away each pay cycle and then deciding how to invest the money in a bewildering

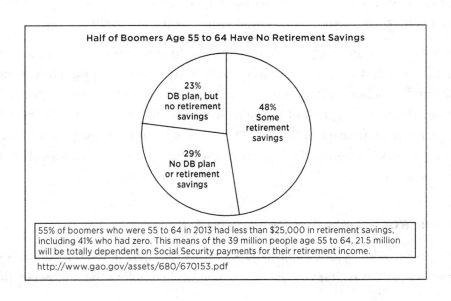

Half of Boomers Age 55 to 64 Have No Retirement Savings

23%
DB plan, but no retirement savings

48%
Some retirement savings

29%
No DB plan or retirement savings

55% of boomers who were 55 to 64 in 2013 had less than $25,000 in retirement savings, including 41% who had zero. This means of the 39 million people age 55 to 64, 21.5 million will be totally dependent on Social Security payments for their retirement income.

http://www.gao.gov/assets/680/670153.pdf

set of choices does not bode well for the future. While 48 percent have some retirement savings, 52 percent of boomers age fifty-five to sixty-four in 2013 had less than $25,000, and 41 percent had zero.

Rather than entering into their retirement years with a sense of financial security, boomers are trying to figure it out as they go. Fifty-nine percent see their best solution is to keep working or never retire, yet only 29 percent of those over sixty-five years old have been able to do so.[52]

The one thing that stands clear about the boomer generation is their rootlessness. Through a quirk in history, they find themselves believing in traditional values but living nontraditional lives. They were raised in a youth culture where they were treated as equals, but because of their numbers, they have found themselves competing against one another in the workforce. Raised in a consumer culture that said, "You can have it all," they found themselves grabbing all they could before their money ran out. They looked for transcendence through drugs, but found that speed kills. Told that they were middle class, many found themselves living in a nation divided between the super-rich and the growing numbers of poor.

Ironically, instead of turning to one another for the values they hold in common, they turned inward to themselves to find meaning and purpose. In the "Portrait of a Generation" survey done by *Rolling Stone*, this generation is described as one "that had retreated into itself" and as one that was "isolationist."[53]

The result of rootlessness is self-seeking: a person shuns the values of the outside world and looks inward to find meaning and purpose. What some have mistakenly labeled as selfishness is instead an inner search for meaning and truth. It is to that search that we will now turn.

CHAPTER
4

Self-Seeking

In 1986 Whitney Houston hit the top of the charts with her song "The Greatest Love of All," a soul-filled rock ballad that personified the credo of the 1980s. The song is not about love in the traditional sense; it is not about romance between two lovers; it is not about God; it is not about brotherhood and sisterhood or giving to humanity. Instead, its message is that the greatest love is inside each person. The song, which portrayed itself as a song of hope and love, holds within it a summation of the philosophy of the boomer generation: after the turmoil of the '60s and the disappointments of the '70s, the only thing that is going to bring meaning to life is learning to love yourself.

What some saw as greed, narcissism, and selfishness, boomers turned to as the natural result of brokenness, loneliness, and rootlessness. It wasn't that the boomer generation had given up on the world. Instead, the individual boomer decided the only person he or she could depend on was himself or herself.

Boomers started coming to this conclusion in the late 1960s and early '70s. As the counterculture, the rock stars of the 1960s, and the student movement faded, this generation turned introspective. Now that the revolution was over, the present had to be filled with meaning. Many of the veterans of the various movements of the '60s found purpose in the human potential movement.

Todd Gitlin says that all the encounter groups, therapies, and mystical disciplines were supposed to help people get down to their real selves. So people learned to "live in the present," to "go with the flow," to "give themselves permission," and to "get in touch with their feelings."[1]

This search for self happened in many unexpected places, and not everyone went through it willingly. I encountered it firsthand in my church youth group in the late '60s and early '70s. One time I remember being put in the middle of a circle and told to express my feelings about each person in the group. I really did not want to do it. I did not know what to say, but as it was the thing to do, I did it anyway.

At another memorable meeting, I was taught to punch pillows to express my anger. It felt weird to be hitting pillows with my friends to express an anger I really did not feel. At a youth camp, our pastor led us in a body awareness exercise where everyone lay on the floor in a line, side by side, and we took turns rolling over one another in an attempt to "find ourselves."

At that time, it seemed as if everyone were on a search for something. Even the adults I knew were starting to do strange things. The parents of two of my friends decided to switch partners, so they divorced and married their newfound lovers. The most popular teacher at my high school divorced his wife, with whom he had two children, and married one of the graduating seniors.

Another friend was taken by his parents with his brother and two sisters to a nudist colony to experience nature. And his father was a pastor. The parents of another friend told me I was a medium and encouraged me to develop my psychic abilities. Another time I attended a meeting of a church member who interpreted our dreams and foretold our futures.

Boomers Rocked by Their Parents' Divorces

Second-wave boomers (born after 1953) bore the brunt of this experimentation by adults. In school, each teacher and school system decided to try new methods and techniques. Boomers went from new math to new English to open classrooms to schools without walls and so on. I always joke that I cannot spell because each year I was taught a new method. If it were not for "spell checkers" on computers, millions of baby boomers would not be able to write a sentence that doesn't have to be deciphered.

Dr. Judith Mack, the director of counseling at the University of California, Davis, in talking about younger boomers when they were in college, commented that her most difficult, therapy-resistant cases came from homes where parents were so caught up in the changes in their own lives that they hardly had time to be parents. Their children were given every monetary advantage, when what they really needed was their parents.[2]

One boomer remembered how her full-time professional mother suddenly lost interest in mothering and decided it was time to find herself. She says, "When I was in junior high, my mother got involved in art and causes. She took a studio and painted and had a lot of artist friends. She was also the head of a lot of committees. What I remember is that she was on the phone all the time."[3] Susan Littwin says:

> It is hard to remember how crazy all of that was. Couples are still divorcing and women, more than ever, are working and having lives outside of their families. But we have institutionalized the change and we go about our lives without guilt. There is day care and after school care and family therapy and joint custody and dozens of other buffers that make it work routinely, if not painlessly. But in the sixties, the breakup of the nuclear family—with mamma at home— exploded on us.[4]

From 1966 to 1976, the divorce rate doubled from 2.5 per thousand to 5.0. The raw numbers went from 499,000 divorces a year in 1966 to 1,083,000 divorces in 1976. During the same period, the marriage rate remained fairly stable, going from 9.5 in 1966 to 10.0 in 1976. Since then, the marriage and divorce rates have stayed fairly constant, at 10.0 for marriage and at 5.0 for divorce.[5]

By combining the figures of divorced single parents, I estimate that between 1966 and 1976 about seventeen million baby boomers went through a divorce with their parents. This would mean that 22 percent or almost one in four baby boomers had parents who went through a divorce. Contrary to the image of boomers as people who had golden childhoods, many boomers went through the emotional hardships that these changes brought about. The first-wave boomers, who were the leaders of social change, stand in contrast to the second- and third-wave boomers who bore the weight of these changes—as seen in their families and in their education at school.

I remember the experience of performing weddings for boomers in the 1980s. About three quarters of the weddings I performed contained two elements. First, the couple that was getting married had been living together. Sometimes one of them was divorced and had a child. The second element was divorced parents. It was interesting to see how couples handled these two elements. With respect to the first, the couple who had been living together thought nothing of it. They did not see anything unusual in their premarital arrangement. They did not regard their lifestyle as sinful, which is what people in the 1950s would surely have thought. What caused them embarrassment was their parents.

As we talked about the wedding ceremony, the question would come up, "What do I do about my parents?" One bride echoed the feelings of many boomers: "They're divorced, and my mother will be there with my stepfather, and my father will be there with his girlfriend. Where will they sit, and whom should I ask to give me away? I think my father should give me away. But my mother and stepfather have raised me since I was about twelve, so I actually feel closer to my stepfather. But if he gives me away, my father will be hurt."

Questions such as these had nothing to do with etiquette. These questions had to do with processing what had happened in their families and trying to make sense out of what remained. One of my early experiences in ministry, in 1979, was helping a high-school senior deal with the divorce of her parents. Without warning, her mother left her father to live with a boyfriend from work. This young boomer was angry, shocked, ashamed, and hurt all at the same time. I distinctly remember one of her remarks: "They both got lawyers, and last night they were fighting over who was going to keep an umbrella. Actually, it's my umbrella. As far as I'm concerned, my mother can take the umbrella and shove it. I don't want it any more. I'll go get my own damn umbrella."

The relationship between boomers and their parents has a lot to do with self-seeking. Even the name of the sixties movement that causes the most soul-searching in the area of personal values and appearance—"the counterculture"—retained in it the element of adolescent rebellion against parental authority. After all, what good would it do to grow long hair if your parents did not complain about it?

Midge Decter, a mother of boomers, notes that boomers did things that were designed to provoke some kind of reaction from their parents. Raised as children in the middle class, boomers were expected to be well dressed; therefore, they "dressed themselves in rags." Raised with the expectation of being well groomed and healthy, they "cultivated the gaudiest show of slovenliness and the most unmistakable signs of sickliness." Raised on the premise that they would be prompt and well mannered, they "compounded a group style based on nothing so much as a certain weary, breathless vagueness and incompetence enriched by the display of a deep, albeit soft spoken, disrespect for the sensibilities and concerns of others."

Directing her comments to boomers, Decter wrote:

That key to this assertion of style lay in an exact reverse translation of what your parents had taken for granted on your behalf is only one mark of how necessary we were in all your efforts to define yourselves with the main issue for you so obviously being not "what in my own mature opinion will be best for me?" but "what will they think or how will they feel in the face of this present conduct of mine?"[6]

When I was in college, I drove my parents crazy by answering their question of what I wanted to do with my future by answering, "I'm just taking it one day at a time. God will take care of me." Yet the reality was that my parents were taking care of me—paying my tuition to college and providing for my housing, food, and car insurance. At that time, it didn't dawn on me that their real question was, "When are you going to become an adult?"

There is an irony in all of this. Because their parents took such good care of them, providing them with everything they needed—food, housing, consumer goods, cars, education, and all that went with it—many boomers never really wanted to grow up. In 1972, sociologist James S. Coleman had discerned the regressive character of the burgeoning new youth culture: "Locked into a world of their own creation, their own music and money and a license to do as they wished the young saw no reason to abandon this 'pleasing surrogate for maturity.'"[7]

Kenneth L. Woodward wrote in an article on "Young Beyond Their Years":

Adolescence is a period of intense self-absorption—a time for finding out who you are and the sort of person you can and ought to become. Adulthood, on the other hand, implies the development of character, competence and commitment, qualities essential for self-discipline, cooperation and taking care of others. By these standards, young Americans entering the 21st century are far less mature than their ancestors were at the beginning of the 20th. The difference is evident in all areas of youthful development: sex, love, marriage, education, and work.[8]

The result for third-wave boomers was that many of them had a hard time cutting the apron strings from mom and dad. One of the surprising developments of the 1980s was the number of boomers who went back home. It was not uncommon to find boomers who went to college and, after giving it a try in the workforce, came back home to live with their parents when they did not make it. Another common situation was the divorced single mother returning home with children to live with her parents.

I know of one merged family consisting of two parents and ten boomer children. When they got them all out of the house, they drew a deep breath. Wanting to move up in life, the parents contracted to build a beautiful four-bedroom house in which they thought they would spend the golden years of their retirement. But to their surprise, the children suddenly needed to move back in with them. For two years, they never had the house to themselves. One child had a drug problem and had to live with them. After they helped him through the problem and got him on his feet, another child went through a divorce and needed a place to stay. When she moved out, another daughter with her husband and two children moved in. They had sold their old house and misjudged the time it would take for the construction to be finished on their new one.

So, when the husband had a heart attack, the older couple immediately made a decision. In one month, they sold the new house and bought a condo with one nice master bedroom and a small bedroom, which they set up as an office. In effect, they made it impossible for the children to move home. They would no longer be available to bail out the kids when they got in trouble. As the mother said, "It just got to be too much. We need to be able to have our own lives. They have to make it on their own. We won't take care of them; they're adults, not children anymore."

The Dependence Trap

This inability of some boomers to overcome their dependence on their parents is a reflection of a number of elements that affect the way boomers see themselves and live their lives. Furthermore, as boomers became parents, many of them turned their dependence on their parents to dependence on their children.

Mom, a comedy on CBS, is a popular hit because it rings so true. Anna Faris plays Christy Plunkett, a single young-adult mother who struggles with drugs and gambling as she tries to raise her two children. The focus of the show is on her relationship with her mom, Bonnie.

Bonnie is the prototype boomer who miserably failed as a mother when Christy was growing up. Now that she has recovered from her own addictions through therapy, she has found peace and wants to have the relationship with her daughter she never had when Christy was a child.

Allison Janney, who won the Emmy in 2015 for her role as Bonnie, thanked the creator of the show for "creating such a deeply flawed character and immediately thinking of me to play her." She added, "So many lives are touched by addiction and it is a privilege to work on a show that reminds us there is hope."[9]

While *Mom* focuses on the boomer parents who never got it together, on the flipside are the boomer parents whose goal in life is to manage their children's lives to ensure they are a success. Or to make sure they don't mess up like they did.

Rather than letting go of their children when they go to college, they persist in having a say in every decision their children try to make. In extreme cases, they try to influence their children's professors or employers to fix a perceived wrong.

College campuses are experiencing an influx of students who are so ill-prepared for the real world that they can't handle getting a bad grade. These students don't know how to deal with a roommate who bugs them. They feel pressured to be perfect because of how much their parents have done for them. Raised by parents who have intervened on behalf of their children throughout their lives, these children do not have the tools to make it on their own. Peter Gray in "Declining Student Resilience: A Serious Problem for Colleges," says,

> We have raised a generation of young people who have not been given the opportunity to learn how to solve their own problems. They have not been given the opportunity to get into trouble and find their own way out, to experience failure and realize they can survive it, to be called bad names by others and learn how to respond without adult intervention. So now, here's what we have: Young people, 18 years and older, going to college still unable or unwilling to take responsibility for themselves, still feeling that if a problem arises they need an adult to solve it.[10]

So what factors have led to so many boomers to this state of being? First, they are the product of the consumer culture that has taught them their life is validated not by who they are but by what they have. Thousands of commercials have filled their minds with the message of consumerism: meaning and purpose are found in what you wear, what you drive, where you live, and what you can afford.

The second element is living for the present. The first generation raised under the threat of nuclear annihilation, they learned to treat each moment as their last. There is little sense of history or future in the lives of boomers. In the business world, the goal is short-term profits rather than long-range planning. In personal life, the goal is "going with the flow" and "living it up."

The one thing that surprises many boomers today is they have made it this far. It's not unheard of for a member of this generation to say, "If I had known I was going to live this long, I would have done a better job of getting ready for it."

The third factor is instant gratification. Boomers want what they want *now*. The whole culture reflects this. In an age of huge government deficit spending and living on credit, commercials remind us during the Christmas season, "You don't have to pay till March." Today's smartphones with their sophisticated apps promise instant access to all the information in the world. Every friend and relative is believed to be just one text away. Any product you want—from books to clothes to toys for a grandchild to groceries—is now one click away on Amazon.

The fourth element is the trivialization of culture. Everything is marketable and sellable. When the Berlin Wall fell in late 1989, pieces of it were sold in stores during the Christmas season. Pepsi featured commercials showing the Berlin Wall and proclaiming "Peace on Earth" printed underneath the Pepsi logo.

What was a moving historical event affecting the lives of millions of Europeans who were finding freedom was made into part of an ad campaign and sold in stores like pet rocks.

In a culture that trivializes historical events, little value is placed on things that last. The association of the images with a product or with a need to buy the latest fad denigrates whatever emotion is elicited by images that move the soul. The end result is rampant escapism, evident all across American culture. The slogan "escape to the movies" sums up what millions of Americans hope to do through a great variety of means.

From the workaholic who wants to escape from the family to the drug addict who seeks relief from the burdens of life to the sports fan who lives and dies with his favorite fantasy team on *FanDuel* to the Toys R Us kid who sings, "I don't want to grow up . . . ," to the hedonist who finds relief in the pleasures of the flesh, to the stargazer who revels in the scandals and troubles of a favorite celebrity, to the traditionalist who tries to go back to "the way it was," to the young-at-any-cost who exercises the body to skin and bones or alters the body through cosmetic surgery, boomers have found a slew of ways to flee the realities of life, to negate the changing panorama of the world, to insulate themselves from the ravages of time, to avoid dealing with their own mortality.

The Paradox of Self-Seeking

The focus on the now and the desire to escape has led people into the curious paradox of self-seeking. Thinking that one is free to choose one's own life, to be an authentic human being, one becomes dependent on others to define the self. Without a cultural history or family tradition afforded by the extended family of the past, the twenty-first-century citizen is dependent on experts and advisors to lead the way.

It is no accident that boomers seek constant advice from self-help books, YouTube videos, and celebrity experts like Dr. Oz to navigate their daily lives. From dealing with young-adult children who are living in their homes, to learning to love, to coping with spouses who cheat, to managing a business, to curing a baffling array of illnesses, to taking care of an aging parent, to becoming rich—a whole corps of self-helpers are there to ease boomers through the messy and complicated labyrinth of life.

In *The Culture of Narcissism*, Christopher Lasch wrote:

Narcissism represents the psychological dimension of this dependence. Notwithstanding his occasional illusions of omnipotence, the narcissist depends on others to validate his self-esteem. He cannot live without an admiring audience. His apparent freedom from his family ties and institutional constraints does not free him to stand alone or to glory in his individuality. On the contrary, it contributes to his insecurity, which he can overcome only by seeing his "grandiose self" reflected in the attentions of others, or by attaching himself to those who radiate celebrity, power, and charisma. For the narcissist, the world is a mirror, whereas the rugged individualist saw it as an empty wilderness to be shaped to his own design.[11]

This endless looking in the mirror at one's own reflection carries with it a heavy burden—boredom. There is only so much navel gazing a person can do. How many tummy tucks and how much analysis can people undergo before they realize that they are not so unique after all? Boomers are getting older and are facing the realization that they are not mythical gods free to do as they please for all eternity. But, in fact, they are mortal beings who face the reality of life and death.

Most boomers resist the idea of retirement because the idea of life without the structure of work is a scary proposition. Once they leave the workforce, what are they going to do?

This is not to say that everything about boomer self-seeking is wrong. In *The Denial of Death*, Ernest Becker notes that in humans "a working level of narcissism is inseparable from self-esteem, from a basic sense of self-worth."[12]

But self-worth is not created in a vacuum; it does not happen spontaneously. It happens as a result of one's interactions with the world in which one finds meaning and purpose. It is found in the symbols of meaning with which we surround ourselves. It is seen in what we create and offer to the world.

Thus Steven Jobs, a boomer born in 1955, could start Apple Computer in his garage at the age of twenty and propel it into a multimillion-dollar business on the strength of symbols and visionary ideas. Jobs's goal was to "change the world."

Michael Murray, who was recruited out of Stanford University in 1980, remembers the messianic aura that surrounded Jobs, as he unblushingly believed Apple Computer offered the dream of remaking the world through the personal computer.

"This was the psychology of Mac. This was its passion," he says. "We believed fundamentally that we were changing the world. We honestly did. What Apple represented was the democratization of technology. Putting this enormously powerful thing called technology, which can be so scary, into the hands of the people."

"Most of us were in our late twenties and early thirties," says Murray. "We missed the Beatles. We missed the civil rights movement. We missed Vietnam. Macintosh was our social revolution. We threw ourselves into it."[13]

In this way, the narcissism and self-seeking of boomers marks not only a peculiar problem, but also a special point of spiritual challenge, quest, and opportunity. For all of their narcissism, boomers seek what others have sought through other commitments and dreams—a place of meaning and purpose. They seek to be heroes in their own story, and in the world as they see it.

Dorothy as the Prototype Boomer

There is no accounting for the influence of *The Wizard of Oz* on the psyche of the boomer generation. Unlike today when you can stream it online or watch it on a DVD or Blu-ray Disc whenever you want, when I was a child, the movie was shown once a year on CBS. I was excited, because I was allowed to stay up late to watch the whole thing. I remember watching it with my cousins and sisters and thought it was always shown on a holiday.

As a teenager, I remember singing the songs with my friends at camp and doing the "Yellow Brick Road" dance, walking with our arms intertwined. When we were scared, we would say, "Lions and tigers and bears, oh my!" Even in college, sometimes my fellow dormies and I would reenact some of the highlights of *The Wizard of Oz*. I never remember anyone doing the same thing with other childhood tales, such as Peter Pan or Cinderella.

Although the story of *The Wizard of Oz* seems to cherish the values of home and family, it is actually a story about a girl who has to make it on her own, who by accident becomes the heroine of the Munchkins. The most important scenes have to do with Dorothy's interaction with the Wizard of Oz, who she believes will solve all her problems and enable her to go home. But in the end, as Dorothy stands alone, abandoned by the Wonderful Wizard of Oz, she wonders if anyone can help her. It is only through the wisdom of the Good Witch that she is able to return from the colorized world of Oz to the black and white world of Kansas when she is told that she had to power to go home within herself.

The story of Dorothy in the Land of Oz is a powerful myth for the boomer generation because it echoes so much of their experience of self-seeking. Madonna Kolbenschlag in *Lost in the Land of Oz* says, "As an adult woman I found in Dorothy a mythic symbol that resonated with many of the turning points in my own growth to moral maturity—most of which would be described as acts of rebellion. No longer was she a childhood fantasy figure, but suddenly she took on a more heroic aspect. Especially in her encounters with the Wizard Dorothy seemed to portray so much of the reality of our experience of awakening and of seizing our own inner authority and autonomy as women."[14]

In *The Wizard of Oz* we see many predecessors to the movements that would affect boomers and their search for fulfillment and meaning. In Dorothy, we find the empowered woman who finds herself; in the Tin Man, Scarecrow, and Lion, we find the bumbling men who find meaning by chasing after degrees and medals; in the Bad Witch and the Good Witch, we see an acceptance of a belief system outside of Christianity; in the rainbow, we find the symbol of the New Age Movement and later the Gay Rights

Movement; in the Emerald City, we find the escapism that dominates much of our culture; and in the Wizard, we find the failure of institutions to keep their promises.

One thing that makes Dorothy such an attractive heroine to boomers is the fact that she is an orphan, the abandoned one who has to find herself. There is within her journey a sense of not being a part of this world, of being just a visitor, not a complete participant. Her whole purpose is to return home, but even home is lacking a father and a mother.

As much as she might love her aunt, there is no replacing the security and love of a parent. Perhaps more than anything else, it is this feeling of lostness that captures the imagination of boomers. For it is only when we recognize our lostness in the modern-day world of Oz that we begin to find meaning in life. Madonna Kolbenschlag has captured the weight of this feeling.

> In spite of the illusion that partners, family, clan, nation, or church project in my life, my reality is that I am needy, love-starved, lonely, frightened of what may happen; I am bereft of models and mentors, detached from my history and roots, longing for connection. Only when I have accepted the reality of my orphan self, can I begin to really live.[15]

The net result of all this is that boomers experience a great deal of ambivalence in their quest for meaning and purpose. Longing for home, family, and connection, they nevertheless feel compelled by brokenness, rootlessness, and loneliness to depend only upon themselves or the power of their efforts to find the end of the rainbow. Boomers spend a lot of energy trying to escape this deep sense of conflict. Most of the time, these feelings are not even recognized. In quiet moments of reflection, many would admit to wanting to *get away*, if only for a moment, to find some kind of peace in a world that is running at warp speed.

The challenge for the boomer generation is that they live in a culture that thrives on change, a world that is driven by trends, that eats up cultural identities and spits them out in a more palatable dish called "American."

The reality is that America is built on rootlessness, loneliness, and brokenness. The person who is not willing to break with family, to move to a new city and face loneliness, and to pull up roots and try something new will have difficulty making it in a competitive world that thrives on innovation and change.

Bruce Jenner's interview in the spring of 2015 with Diane Sawyer (at which point he was still using male pronouns) about his decision to become a woman was the quintessential boomer moment. It brought into focus the interplay between the values of brokenness, loneliness, rootlessness, and self-seeking.

As he described his life story, the worldview of his generation was clearly articulated. Since he was eight years old, he had felt a sense of brokenness that who he was on the outside was not who he was on the inside. Even when he won the decathlon in the 1976 Olympics and was crowned the World's Greatest Athlete, he knew he did not meet the expectations of a society that expected him to be a man's man.

During his three marriages and even after fathering six children, he was filled with loneliness because he didn't think anyone would understand him. Although he was attracted to women, he felt that he was a female inside. He also concluded that therapy wasn't the answer. How could you change the way you were born? He said he was a deeply religious man and when God made him, God decided to give him a curve ball. He would have the physical attributes of a man that made him one of the world's best athletes but have a female brain.

His brokenness and loneliness led to a sense of rootlessness, of not finding safe sanctuary in a world that did not understand or accept who he was. But now that he was sixty-five, he wasn't going to wait any longer. In an ultimate decision of self-seeking, he was going to undertake a year of surgeries and treatments to become who he was meant to be: a woman. Then he articulated a statement that perfectly summarizes what drives many boomers to make transformative decisions: "This is going to help thousands of people."

Caitlin Jenner's understanding of herself and her worldview should be a wake-up call to any organization, corporation, or group that provides goods and services to boomers. When Diane Sawyer asked why at sixty-five years of age, one would make this decision, Jenner replied, "I could come down with a fatal disease at any time and be dead in a couple of years. I don't have time to wait. If I want to become the person I was meant to be, I have to do it now."[16]

I doubt there are many people of previous generations who would take this view. Previous generations of older adults did not expect to live twenty to thirty years after their retirement. The ultimate goal was to retire to a place like The Villages in Florida where you could golf until you died or to buy a Winnebago and travel the country with all the comforts of home.

Boomers, who have always been driven by a sense of destiny that they were going to change the world, are not planning to go quietly into the night. After all, when they were young, they challenged the government to stop the Vietnam War. They were early adopters of the civil rights movement and the women's rights movement. As adults, they even helped elect the first African American president.

Boomers are heading into their older-adult years with a sense of urgency. If they have been waiting to make dramatic changes in their lives, now will be the time to do it. They will not be content to sit in a senior center playing bingo or going on church tours to museums. They will gravitate to churches and organizations that are changing communities for the better, and they will champion causes that are important to them. They will be on a quest for self-improvement that will rival the days of their youth, when with a restless spirit, they dropped acid, hitchhiked across Europe, and meditated as if they were from Tibet.

Many boomers display antipathy toward the American culture. By its very nature, the pursuit of the perfect life brings people to a point of isolation. Until individuals of this generation face their lostness in this world and admit that they are orphans facing an uncertain future, they will continue to try to escape. For when a person truly finds self, that person finds an orphan self. Even Jesus on the cross modeled the lostness of the orphan when he said, "My God, my God, why have you forsaken me?" (Matt. 27:46, NRSV). Strangely enough, it is when one comes to this realization that one finds hope. In the acceptance of brokenness, loneliness, and rootlessness, a person is able to go beyond self-seeking to search for God.

PART
2

The Search for God

Jesus Christ Superstar,
Do you think you're what they say you are?

"Superstar," Andrew Lloyd Webber and Tim Rice,
Jesus Christ Superstar, A Rock Opera, 1970

CHAPTER
5

Godliness

It was unexpected. Like everything else the boomers embraced, it was unconventional, anti-institutional, emotional, experiential, and deeply personal. The chroniclers of the 1960s youth movement were caught off-guard, yet they reported it with the zeal they did with every other movement the boomers got caught up in. Their parents were at once touched and troubled, for even though it embraced some of their most cherished beliefs, it challenged their lifestyles at a level much deeper than the hippie movement ever could. The boomers turned on to Jesus.

I remember my experience with it. I was in eighth grade in May 1968. A lay witness team came to our church to witness to us about faith in Jesus Christ. I had never heard this message before, at least not presented in this way. They said, "Jesus was a personal savior who died on the cross to forgive you of your sins." They said things like, "I love you and God loves you" and "Even if you were the only person who ever lived on this earth, Jesus still would have given his life for you so you could be saved."

This powerful message hit me at a time when I was most in need of love. I had done nothing exceptional in my life. I was a short teenager with red hair and freckles, glasses and braces, all the things that the Marlboro man was not. I was a good son, raised by loving parents, and had grown up in The Methodist Church but had not found anything that touched my heart.

I was a *Wonder Years'* kid, who watched the older members of my generation go off to war or to hippiedom while I was still trying to figure out how to get rubber bands to stay on my braces. But it was at just that moment of my greatest vulnerability and need that I heard the message that Jesus loved me.

On a Sunday morning while the adults were in worship in the sanctuary, the youth were worshiping in the chapel. During our service, the leader had an altar call, something that was completely foreign to my religious experience. While "How Great Thou Art" was being played on the organ, I went forward and accepted Jesus Christ. As I knelt on the floor, I said, "Dear Lord, I give my life to you to do as you will."

I will never forget that moment. Like a current of power, I felt the Spirit of God fill my heart. My friends also felt it, and as a group we raised ourselves from our knees and rushed into the main sanctuary and fell before the altar and prayed.

Of course, the adults were shocked. The guest speaker was in the middle of his sermon, and here were twenty of their children weeping and crying right in the middle of the altar area. I do not know exactly what they did with us. Somehow the worship service was completed, and we finished the day with a farewell potluck for the lay mission group. But the aftermath of that experience sums up the problem many boomers faced with their passion for religious experience.

When we came back the next Sunday, the youth wanted to do something about the experience, but our parents were caught in a quandary. Our pastor, who had been gone the previous week, preached the same old sermon and was not comfortable with this kind of "religious emotionalism." Parents who had been made very uncomfortable by the passionate outburst of their children were trying to figure out how to handle this "experience." They hoped it was a fad or something that would pass with time.

Of course, on a deeper level, it challenged their beliefs in a God who was very logical, rational, upright, and socially acceptable. The biggest problem with the passionate response was that it looked like something only Holy Rollers would do, praying and singing and crying about their love for Jesus.

The Mainline Church's 50s Mentality Shut Out Many Boomers

For years, the mainline Protestant churches had done their best to separate themselves from the fundamentalists, the evangelicals, and especially the Pentecostal churches. Embracing the theology of neo-orthodoxy and preaching the social gospel, these churches hit their heyday in the mid-1960s. In 1965, the Presbyterian Church with 4.3 million and the United Church of Christ with 2 million members reached their highest recorded membership. In 1965, the Methodist Church with 11 million in the United States, the Episcopal Church with 3.4 million, and the Disciples of Christ with 1.9 million, each recorded its highest membership in history. But by 2010, these denominations had lost 35 percent of their combined membership, going from 30.2 million in 1965 to 19.7 million in 2010, a loss of more than 10.4 million members.[1]

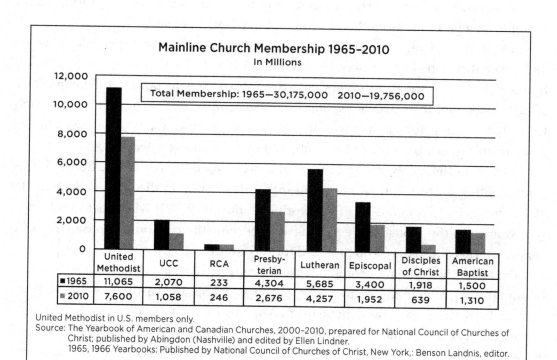

Mainline Church Membership 1965–2010
In Millions

Total Membership: 1965—30,175,000   2010—19,756,000

	United Methodist	UCC	RCA	Presbyterian	Lutheran	Episcopal	Disciples of Christ	American Baptist
■1965	11,065	2,070	233	4,304	5,685	3,400	1,918	1,500
■2010	7,600	1,058	246	2,676	4,257	1,952	639	1,310

United Methodist in U.S. members only.
Source: The Yearbook of American and Canadian Churches, 2000-2010, prepared for National Council of Churches of Christ; published by Abingdon (Nashville) and edited by Ellen Lindner.
1965, 1966 Yearbooks: Published by National Council of Churches of Christ, New York,: Benson Landnis, editor.

Their collective loss of members since 1965 is a reflection of their inability to keep and to attract the boomer generation. It is ironic that the churches that were the most supportive of the civil rights movement, who were on the cutting edge of the feminist movement, who battled for inclusive language, and who were the most active in supporting human rights are now the churches that are hurting the most. Why is it that as boomers searched for God, they found the most powerful churches of the '50s and '60s to be wanting? By answering this question, we will go a long way in understanding the boomers' desire for godliness.

By all standards, the 1950s in America was a unique decade in the history of the nation. First, the United States economy dominated the world. It is hard to remember that, in the '50s, Japan, China, and Europe were in ruins, devastated from the battles of World War II. It would take fifty years for them to fully recover. The only other power Americans had to fear was the Soviet Union, whose threat came in the form of the power to wage war and from their technological advances in space.

But the Soviet Union was always a poor competitor in the world of consumer goods and never threatened the American consumer market. As a result of this economic boom of the '50s, American workers had extraordinary buying power. As Martha Farnsworth Riche says in an article in *American Demographics*, "For the first and probably the only time in history, a man with less than average education could afford a house, two cars in the garage, three or four kids, and a non-working wife."[2]

Second, in the 1950s, it was believed that women's place was in the home. Rather than building on the gains women had made after winning the right to vote in the 1920s and being the mainstay of the workforce during WWII when men went off to war, women in the 1950s were encouraged to become the traditional housewives who supported their husbands who provided for the family.

The belief that a woman could be fulfilled only by having a family fueled the baby boom. The birthrate climbed to twenty-seven per thousand in the mid-1950s. From 1945 to 1946, there was a jump in births in America from 2,873,000 to 3,426,000. Each successive year added more births until 1954, when the total went to 4,102,000 and stayed over 4,000,000 each year until 1964.[3] In 1957, when births hit an all-time record high of 4.3 million, proud census officials pointed out that in 1957 one baby was born

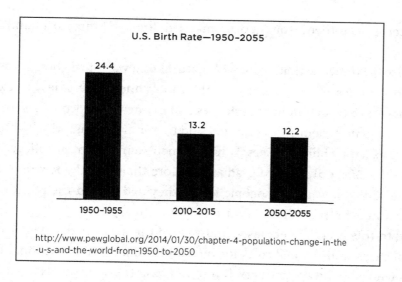

U.S. Birth Rate—1950-2055

http://www.pewglobal.org/2014/01/30/chapter-4-population-change-in-the-u-s-and-the-world-from-1950-to-2050

every seven seconds. From 1950 to 1955, the U.S. birthrate was 24.4 per thousand. This is sharp contrast to the birthrate of 13.2 from 2010 to 2015 and future projections of 12.2 in 2050–2055.[4]

What made this unusual was that in most other Western countries, after a brief baby boom following the war, the birthrate dropped. Only Canada, Australia, and New Zealand kept up with the high rate of the United States. So high was this birthrate that it rivaled and sometimes surpassed the birthrate of underdeveloped countries, where the much talked about population explosion was taking place.[5]

Adding to the baby boom was the huge number of teenage marriages. In 1953, almost a third of American females had married by the time they reached 19. The median age at first marriage dropped from 25.9 for males and 21.9 for females in 1900 to an all-time low of 22.8 for males and 20.3 for females in the mid-1950s.[6] In 1900, 48 percent of women age 20 to 24 were married. By 1960 71 percent of women age 20 to 24 were married.[7]

This is in sharp contrast to today's reality. In 1960, 88 percent of people age 25 to 34 were married. By 2014, only 51 percent of people age 25 to 34 were married. Two major concerns keep them from getting married: financial insecurity and finding the right person.[8]

In the 1950s, the view that a woman's natural role was in the home was expressed by educated Americans and taught in high schools and universities as scientific fact. While men were to be taught in the sciences and mathematics, women were best suited for courses in home economics, ceramics, and flower arranging, which prepared them for their role as happy homemakers. While women's enrollment in college almost doubled during the '50s, only a third graduated. More than half the female students who dropped out did so because, as people joked, they had gained their MRS degree and were now working on their Ph.T., "Putting Hubby Through."[9]

Adding to this was the persuasive message of the mass media, which was a prime purveyor of these well-defined roles for men and women. On television, Lucy was the zany housewife who always got herself into impossible situations. Harriet Nelson was the perfect wife and mother who stayed at home. Alice Kramden was the battling wife who was always caught up in one household chore or another.

Women's magazines, which were a powerful force in the '50s, pushed this stereotypical image with articles such as "How to Snare a Male," "Should I Stop Work When I Marry?," "Are You Training Your Daughter to Be a Wife?," "Really a Man's World, Politics," "Femininity Begins at Home," "Have Babies When You're Young," and "The Business of Running a Home."

This need to stay within prescribed roles leads us to the third unique characteristic of the '50s, which was the need for conformity. As the economy prospered and as men returned from the war, there was a mass migration from the country to the city. As men expanded their horizons, they moved where industries provided jobs, and they moved from the farm to the suburbs. Although boomers may long for the traditional family life of the '50s, the parents of boomers experienced the '50s as a great time of transition. People who had been raised on farms or in small towns found themselves in teeming neighborhoods of families. In Los Angeles the first freeway was built, and for the first time men "commuted" to work, which is something as natural to us as having a computer in the office.

Separated from their extended families, which had supported them in the past, the adults of the '50s joined clubs, played bridge, volunteered in community organizations, and went to church. Unlike the boomer generation, their parents were joiners who wanted to belong, who needed to find a sense of community.

While it might be fashionable to deride the choices the mothers of boomers made to raise their children and not go into the workforce, the reality is they didn't just sit around the house and do nothing. Once their children started school, they became the largest volunteer force America had ever seen. They were the heart and soul of churches and had record numbers in groups like the United Methodist Women, who raised millions of dollars for mission work and social action in the 1960s and 1970s. They were Sunday school teachers, and they headed the PTA at local schools. They were the leaders of women's clubs and garden clubs, and they worked for charitable organizations such as Goodwill and the Salvation Army.

About five years ago, I had lunch with my mom and her friends from her church. They were all in their early nineties, and they had worked together on many church activities over the years. Suddenly, one of her friends called the group to attention, and they began their meeting. They talked about who was in the hospital and needed a visit. They passed around get-well cards for everyone to sign. As they continued their discussions, I got a glimpse of what they must have been like in their prime. This was a formidable group whose focus was on working together to raise money for missions, to support the work of the church, to send members to volunteer in soup kitchens. They paid attention to the needs of their fellow members and their families. Although the majority of them never worked outside the home, their contributions to churches and civic organizations greatly influenced the nature of their communities and neighborhoods.

These three factors—a growing economy, well-defined roles for men and women, and a need to belong—created the fuel for the growth and dominance of the mainline church. During the late '50s, Methodists started one new congregation every three days, and Baptists started one every five days. In 1957, the U.S. Census reported that 96 percent of Americans cited a specific religious affiliation when asked, "What is your religion?"

In the atmosphere of the cold war and McCarthyism, it was considered patriotic to be a Protestant, Catholic, or Jew, as opposed to the anti-God, atheistic communists. In

1954, President Dwight D. Eisenhower said, "Our government makes no sense unless it is founded on a deeply felt religious faith—and I don't care what it is."[10]

This attitude expressed by the president, of not caring what the religious faith of people was as long as they had it, was one of the chief characteristics of 1950s-style religion. Rather than stressing the need for a particular brand of faith, religion was expressed as a transdenominational message, which stressed peace of mind and confident living. Rather than probing the social ills of society and fighting racism, materialism, and sexism, this "faith in faith" mentality was carefully mixed with Freudian insights and depth psychology to offer peace and harmony to people who were trying to live in the "age of anxiety."

Best-selling books of the time included *Peace of Mind* by Reformed Rabbi Joshua Loth Liebman, *A Man Called Peter* by Catherine Marshall, and *Peace of Soul* by Monsignor Fulton J. Sheen, who became one of the first TV religious personalities. The leader of the pack was Norman Vincent Peale, a former Methodist turned Congregationalist, whose book *The Power of Positive Thinking* was published in 1952, stayed on top of the bestseller list for 112 consecutive weeks, and sold more copies than any other book except the Bible in 1954.[11] In the preface of his book, Peale gives a summation of his philosophy:

> The powerful principles contained herein are not my invention but are given to us by the greatest Teacher who ever lived and who still lives. This book teaches applied Christianity; a simple yet scientific system of practical techniques of successful living that works.[12]

Peale's approach was not much different from that of Lafayette Ronald Hubbard, who published a best-seller in 1950 called *Dianetics: The Modern Science of Mental Health*. It combined psychology with scientific analysis to help a "preclear," one who is discovering things about herself or himself and who is becoming clear through sessions with a trained auditor, who uses an "E-meter" to cure all psychoses, neuroses, psychosomatic illnesses, coronary diseases, arthritis, and other ailments. Based on the theory of the brain as a perfect calculating machine, Hubbard's work would become a publishing sensation and was a foundational resource for his new religion, Scientology.

Dianetics was touted in magazine ads and on television and radio as the best-selling self-help book ever published.[13]

Another author, Anne Morrow Lindbergh, topped them all in 1955 with her *Gift from the Sea*, a book addressed to housewives who were distraught with the emptiness of their lives. Ignoring specific institutional appeals, she drew on the long American tradition of mysticism to calm the fears of her readers.[14]

In conflict with this generalized approach to religion was the upsurge of revivalism as personified in Billy Graham, which proclaimed the old-time religion based on personal experience and commitment to Christ, a strict code of morality, gospel hymns, and simple preaching. After a tent-meeting revival in Los Angeles in 1949, Graham vaulted into national prominence with his Billy Graham Evangelistic Association, which used all available mass media to promote his evangelical brand of Christianity. Traveling from city to city, Graham held huge outdoor rallies in stadiums across the country, calling on people to make a personal commitment to Jesus Christ.

Unlike the revivalists of the past, such as Dwight L. Moody and Billy Sunday, Billy Graham's constituencies did not come from the old mainline congregations. Instead, his chief support came from conservatives within the larger Protestant denominations or from churches opposed to the ecumenical movement. As successful as he was, Graham's method did not make a significant number of those who made decisions into good churchgoers. Many people who went forward at an altar call in a stadium never made it to worship on Sunday at the local church.

While Norman Vincent Peale was promoting his "success through Christianity" message and Billy Graham was preaching repentance and belief in a personal savior, mainline churches were caught up in something called "Parish Renewal." Seeking to halt the inroads of patriotic piety and success-oriented religion, mainline pastors embraced the liturgical movement and neo-orthodoxy. While by outward appearances mainline denominations were experiencing record-breaking years in membership, worship attendance, sales of religious books, and new church construction, inwardly there were great concerns to be faced. Leonard I. Sweet wrote about the 1950s in an article called "The Modernization of Protestant Religion in America":

Religious and biblical literacy had seldom been lower. Denominational identities were eroded by the forces of public religion, bureaucratization, and modernism's devaluation of tradition. Allegiances were becoming less to denominations than to movements and causes within denominations. The fifties were the triumphant decade for the definition of church membership as going to church rather than being the church, with the individualistic notion of the church as one's private chapel so rampant that gambits had to be devised to thaw the cold wars going on inside the sanctuaries themselves—guest registration pads passed down the pews, "rituals of friendship" during worship, and their more stylish updating in the 1960s as "the kiss of peace."[15]

Ordained ministers in mainline churches were more likely to be seen as counselors than prophets and as caretakers than visionaries. The rigid standards of education required of the ordained minister brought ministerial students into a bewildering array of biblical criticism. These studies aimed to strip away the "myths of the Bible" in order to find the "historical Jesus," thus exposing students to the minimalist theology of neo-orthodoxy, which denied to history or to the world any capacity for divine revelation except when the kerygmatic "moment of faith" took place. Thus ordained ministers were urged by Karl Barth to stand in the pulpit with the Bible in one hand and the daily paper in the other. Sweet says:

> Theologians specialized in hermeneutical and methodological crossword puzzles, whose answers were absorbing to the players but useless to the wider public. . . . After having created a theological rain forest impenetrable to the unguided mind, both theologians and the clergy they trained only reluctantly served as guides to lay persons brave enough to wish to enter.[16]

Along with complex theologies came the liturgical movement, which in the '60s and '70s sought to bring the laity into an experience of worship whose origins could be traced to the romantic religious revival of the nineteenth century in Great Britain and on the continent among both Roman Catholics and Protestants. A high church form of worship was established as the norm, with congregations reading liturgies and pastors leading worship in the style of priests.

In many churches, rather than bringing the laity into a closer experience of worship, the theology of neo-orthodoxy and the high church style of worship separated clergy even further from their congregations. Instead of giving in to "popular" tastes, pastors saw themselves as the harbingers of culture and spirituality to the uneducated masses.

Ironically, while the Catholics headed toward Vatican II with the intent of opening up worship to the laity with the use of vernacular languages, and while the public embraced the simple message of the half-hour sitcom, mainline churches sanctioned a style of worship that relegated the laity into penitent observers of ritual and practice. Of the era of the '50s, church historian Sydney E. Ahlstrom says that the church "failed to meet religious needs." With a large influx of a mobile people who found a social identification in the church, the church "muffed its chance" to change lives. Ahlstrom explains,

> "Put more analytically, the so-called revival led to a sacrifice of theological substance, which in the face of the harsh new realities of the 1960s left both clergy and laity demoralized and confused. . . . Americans began to sense the dawn of a new age in their spiritual history, a time of reorientation and beginning again, in which the past experience and present situation of every tradition would be opened for reexamination."[17]

The first salvo of this reexamination came in 1957 when the National Guard of Arkansas stood off the assault by whites on a few black children in the segregated Central High School of Little Rock. No longer could churches keep the question of racial justice in a closet. It was hard to look past the fact that in America the worship hour on Sunday mornings was the most segregated hour of the week.

With the National Council of Churches playing a leading role, mainline preachers took on the mantle of the prophet of God who condemned the racist practices of society and the church. While the shining moments were in the civil rights marches led by Martin Luther King Jr., mainline church pastors pushed the social gospel to its limits while forgetting the pastoral and spiritual needs of the congregation. It was not unusual to find the pastor-prophet at war with the congregation who grew tired of the pastor's condemnation of their materialistic lifestyles and racist attitudes, while in the name of justice asking for greater benefits and a higher salary.

Even more nerve-racking to the regular church member was the propensity of denominational leaders to take up the banner of all kinds of causes and issues that the church member opposed. In a more subtle brand of elitism, these leaders followed a fashionable leftward bias that looked down on patriotism and manifested itself in empowerment money for causes such as Angela Davis's defense fund ($10,000 from the United Presbyterian Church in the U.S.A. in 1970), for the "Alianza of New Mexico" and James Forman's "Black Manifesto Movement" ($40,000 and $200,000, respectively, from the Episcopal Church in 1969), and the finishing touch, $85,000 from the World Council of Churches in 1978 to the Patriotic Front in Zimbabwe. A *National Review* cartoon showed this bewildering use of church monies by picturing Vietcong General Giap receiving a telegram that read, "The Episcopal Diocese of New York stands shoulder to shoulder with you in your resistance to American aggression."[18]

The Jesus Movement and the Third Great Awakening

Tom Wolfe, the penetrating social commentator and journalist, put it quite bluntly in a passage written in 1982 from "The 'Me' Decade and the Third Great Awakening."

> The key—one and all decided—was to "modernize" and "update" Christianity. So the Catholics gave the nuns outfits that made them look like World War II Wacs. The Protestants set up "beatnik coffee houses" in the church basement for poetry reading and bongo playing. . . . Both the priests and the preachers carried placards in civil rights marches, gay rights marches, women's rights marches, prisoners' rights marches, bondage lovers' rights marches, or any other marches, so long as they might appear hip to the urban young people. In fact, all the strenuous gestures merely made the church look like rather awkward and senile groupies of secular movements. The much-sought-after Urban Young People found the Hip Churchmen to be an embarrassment, if they noticed them at all. What finally started attracting young people to Christianity was something the churches had absolutely nothing to do with: namely the psychedelic or hippie movement. . . .

Today it is precisely the most rational, intellectual, secularized, modernized, updated, relevant religions—all the brave, forward looking Ethical Culture, Unitarian, and Swedenborgian movements of only yesterday—that are finished, gasping, breathing their last. What the Urban Young People want from religion is a little . . . *Hallelujah!* . . . and *talking in tongues!* . . . *Praise God!*[19]

Thus it was quite a shock to find the children of the mainline churches of the 1950s and early '60s turning on to Jesus when they were teenagers and young adults in the late 1960s and '70s. Boomers who had left the institutionalized church in droves now found themselves caught up in an unexpected movement, the Jesus Movement.

In June 1971, the cover of *Time* proclaimed "The Jesus Revolution." In February of the same year, *Look* gave extensive coverage to the movement in an article titled "The Jesus Movement Is Upon Us." It proclaimed that a crusade, a fundamentalist, Christ-as-personal-Savior revival had caught on in California and showed signs that it would sweep East and take the nation by storm. It said the new evangelists were the young, spreading an old-time, Bible-toting, witness-giving kind of faith. With great joy, they told people to turn on to Jesus, as he was coming—soon.[20]

Calvary Chapel of Costa Mesa, California, was at the forefront of the Jesus Revolution. In a two-year period in the mid-'70s, Calvary Chapel performed more than eight thousand baptisms in the Pacific Ocean and was instrumental in bringing more than twenty thousand conversions to the Christian faith. When Chuck Smith became pastor of Calvary Chapel in the late '60s, he saw a flood of hippies and flower children on the beach and was moved to minister to them. The church, which only had twenty-six members, began to grumble when some of the poorly garbed youth started coming to the church. Early in his ministry at Calvary Chapel, Smith told his leaders:

I don't want it ever said that we preach an easy kind of Christian experience at Calvary Chapel. But I also do not want to make the same mistake that the Holiness Church made thirty years ago. Without knowing it, they drove out and lost a whole generation of young people with a negative no-movie, no-dance, no-smoke gospel. Let us at Calvary not be guilty of this same mistake. Instead, let us trust God and emphasize the work of the Holy Spirit within individual lives. It is exciting and much more real and natural to allow the Spirit to dictate change. Let us never be guilty of forcing our Western Christian sub-culture of clean-shaven, short hairstyles or dress on anyone. We want change to come from the inside out. We simply declare that drugs, striving to become a millionaire, or making sports your whole life is not where true fulfillment or ultimate meaning lies. Because the end of all these goals is emptiness and disappointment.[21]

It was pastors such as Chuck Smith who were able to reach boomers with a message of acceptance and love that caused many to find faith in Jesus Christ. Tai Brooke, a baby boomer who had been turned off by "a small-minded judgmentalism" that was often accompanied by a "chilly aloofness" in the churches he attended, turned to Eastern religions because "the love that is so enthrallingly reported in the New Testament church wasn't very evident in those modern churches."

After a long search for God, which took him as far away as India, he found God one Sunday when he walked into Calvary Chapel. Of that day, he says, "I felt an abundant flow of love the moment I walked through the door. There was not even a fleeting hint of judgmentalism here. Rather, I felt a terrific sense of belonging."[22]

The Specter of the Bomb Colors the Worldview of Boomers

Calvary and other leaders of the Jesus Movement also tapped into an element of the boomer mindset that was largely ignored by mainline churches and their parents' generation. The boomers were the first generation raised under the specter of the nuclear bomb. Born one year after the United States dropped two nuclear bombs on Japan in 1945, boomers lived under a cloud of fear that at any moment they could be blown away in the first salvos of World War III or could die a lingering death from the aftereffects of nuclear radiation.

Chellis Glendinning, in *Waking up in the Nuclear Age,* said:

Before I wove the nuclear threat into my personal story, I had no concept of the effect of nuclear weapons on my life. As I explored the question, I realized two points: one, as a Baby Boomer, I had never known a world without nuclear weapons; and two, I had lived my entire life incapable of planning for the future. A perfect expression of the Be Here Now generation, I never seem to think more than a few weeks or months ahead. Now that I have identified this future uncertainty, I am finally able to imagine a future for myself, even though I admit, consciously for the first time, that it might not come to be.[23]

The dark cloud of nuclear annihilation has been a constant companion for those born in the nuclear age. During the '50s and the early '60s, schoolchildren were drilled in nuclear preparedness. During air raid drills, they were taught to cover their heads as they cowered in the hallways of schools across the land in anticipation of a nuclear attack. During the Cuban Missile Crisis, they helped their parents prepare for "the big one" by stocking up on food, and they watched the building of bomb shelters in their backyards.

While today's children have a wide variety of entertainment options, as a kid in the '60s, I remember watching reruns of *The Twilight Zone* and *The Outer Limits*, which made up a large part of my afterschool TV schedule. Many of the episodes focused on end-of-the-world scenarios. Etched into my memory is *The Twilight Zone* episode called "The Shelter," in which neighbors go to war over who is going to stay in a bomb shelter during an apparent nuclear attack.

In the story, one industrious father had heeded the government's advice to build a bomb shelter in case of nuclear attack. Unfortunately, he was the only one in the neighborhood to do so. When word of an impending attack was made known, he quickly gathered his family into his bomb shelter. Soon neighbors started pounding on the door to let them in to save their families. The image of one family being inside the shelter while neighbors banged on the outside and begged to be let in is firmly imprinted on my mind.

The lesson of the nuclear age is that war is not "out there" somewhere: death can be visited on any neighborhood in the world. One unrelenting message of the war on terrorism has been the underlying theme of what would happen if "they" got their hands on a nuclear bomb.

In modern war, no one is immune. No one is safe. Movies such as *Dr. Strangelove,* *Failsafe, The Day After, Testament, Terminator 2,* and books such as *On the Beach* and *Warday* brought home the disturbing message that all it takes is one mistake, one crazy person, or one fouled-up government decision by either side of the nuclear equation and the world could be blown up. One mushroom cloud of mass destruction would stand as testimony to humankind's ability to destroy itself.

As a teenager, I remember going to see *Planet of the Apes*, a movie very popular with boomers. In it, Charlton Heston's spaceship ends up on a planet ruled by apes. Heston's character meets humans who have become the slaves of the apes. His only hope is to find his spaceship so he can escape the planet and go back to Earth. In the last scene of the movie, Heston is riding a horse on a beach as he comes upon a disturbing sight. In anger and despair he exclaims, "Those maniacs—they did it!" As the scene unfolds, we see the Statue of Liberty buried in the sand. The planet of the apes was Earth. Heston had made it home to a world that had blown itself up.

What now seems like a somewhat silly series of movies was one that brought home to boomers the futility of living in the nuclear age. In sequels to the movie, nuclear weapons were a key element. One movie revolved around a group of nuclear survivors who lived in bombed-out New York City. They worshiped a nuclear bomb as a religious icon that promised salvation to its believers. Its symbolic relation to a policy dubbed MAD (Mutual Assured Destruction) by the government did not go unnoticed in the psyche of the boomer generation.

For the most part, boomers have had an ambivalent relationship with the future. It has not been something they have looked forward to or planned for. For them, the future is eons away. If you talk to boomers about planning for their retirement or about Social Security, you usually get a blank expression and a remark such as "Social Security will be long gone before I get there." This negative outlook affects the way boomers look at the environment ("We'll all be wearing gas masks"); education ("We're raising a generation of illiterates"); the family ("We will all be living alone."); and religion ("The church will be dead").

Four Attitudes Born Out of the Nuclear Age

Much of this attitude can be credited to living life in the nuclear age. First, unlike generations who went before them, boomers have no guarantee of a future for themselves or for their children and grandchildren. For the first time in history, humanity has in its hands the means by which to destroy the Earth. This has nothing to do with superstition, religion, or theory—the destruction of Hiroshima assured us of that. Letting loose the nuclear genie has put the world in great peril. In the blink of an eye, mass destruction can rain down on the Earth and wipe out the human race.

Unlike generations before them who saw themselves as passing on the baton of culture to the next generation, boomers have viewed themselves as the last generation. If another generation is to follow, there is a hesitation about passing on a culture that has brought the world to the precipice of annihilation.

Second, instead of being the savior of the world, technology is seen by many as the destroyer of the Earth. For some, it makes much better sense to go back to the earth, to eat natural foods, to eat lower down on the food chain, and to embrace Mother Earth. The animal rights movement and the environmental movement are reactions to the polluting effects of the industrial age. For people involved in these movements, the epitome of technology gone mad is the nuclear bomb.

Third, with no assured future, boomers live for the now, for the present, for the moment. Long-range plans seem futile and irrelevant. What is important is to make it today. After all, why save for the future if there is not going to be one? Why not build up a big deficit, if we are never going to have to pay it off? Why think about being with someone for fifty years, if the world is going to end in ten?

Fourth, and most important, the dominant view of the future is apocalyptic: the end of the world is at hand. This apocalyptic view of the future is found in many different sources. The best-selling book in the 1970s, with more than twenty-five million copies in print, was a 180-page paperback with the startling title *The Late Great Planet Earth*, written by Hal Lindsey. With its end-of-the-world motif, this book proved to be a perfect match for boomers who expected the end to come at any moment.

In the pages of his book, Lindsey painted a picture of the last judgment according to his interpretation of the book of Revelation and apocalyptic prophecies found in the Old Testament. Central to this scenario was the second coming of Jesus Christ that would happen in our lifetime. After a great war in Israel, the antichrist would emerge as a great leader who would engage in a seven-year period of total war to claim world domination.

Of this period, Lindsey warned that there would be no advantage to being alive. On the stage of world history, this would be the greatest holocaust brought about by the cruelest tyrant of all time.[24]

But would everyone have to suffer? Lindsey said no, there was a way out. You did not have to be here during the seven years of tribulation. According to Lindsey's interpretation of the Bible, there would be one generation that would never know death. Of this generation, those who believed in Jesus Christ would escape the great tribulation, the worst bloodshed, disease, and starvation the world would ever know.[25]

How would they avoid the tribulation? Through the "rapture," the ultimate trip, which offered the promise of three great miracles. First, believers would not die; instead, they would be snatched up from Earth to be with Jesus. Second, they would miss the tribulation and only return to Earth with Christ after the seven-year period of darkness. Third, with Christ they would help usher in the new millennium, a period of one thousand years, during which believers would repopulate the earth under the rule of Christ. At the end of this millennial period, unbelievers would lead a rebellion against Christ, and then Christ would create a new heaven and a new earth.[26]

In the '70s, many boomers fully embraced this view of prophecy. Cars were covered with bumper stickers, such as the one that said: "Warning: If the rapture comes, this car will be unmanned."

A Thief in the Night, a popular movie shown in churches around the country about the rapture, portrayed believers being snatched up out of cars, showers, and the United States Congress without warning, leaving the rest of the world to wonder what had happened to their friends and neighbors.

Twenty years later, this same scenario was featured in the popular *Left Behind* series written by Tim LaHaye and Jerry B. Jenkins that chronicled the results of the rapture in all its bloody detail. The first of the sixteen-book series was published in 1995. By the year 2000, each new book of the series made it to the top of the best-seller lists, and more than sixty-five million copies were sold.[27]

This view of a great escape from the problems of the world has proven to be a perfect match for a generation that has never wanted to grow up. What better answer for fears about death and nuclear war than the one Lindsey and the *Left Behind* series proposed?

Through the rapture, a believer would be beamed up like a character from *Star Trek* and would get to watch the events of the tribulation from the safety of heaven. After the horrible events were over, the believer would return to a world ruled by Christ. This solution offered no mess, no fuss, and best of all, no suffering.

The Message of the Jesus Movement

The Jesus Movement gained traction because it personified what boomers had been looking for all along—a personal experience of godliness that said, "I am important," "I count," "Jesus loves me." Not finding this message in mainline American religion, boomers started their own nondenominational churches or lived in Christian communes or infiltrated established churches in the hope of saving their parents' generation.

Perhaps the most important religious event of the early '70s was the opening of the controversial rock opera *Jesus Christ Superstar* on Broadway in 1971. It was the first Broadway musical ever to have grown from an LP album that sold in the millions before its opening. Written by Andrew Lloyd Webber, then age twenty-three, and Tim Rice, then age twenty-six, the opera was a nonstop, pulsating, rock 'n' roll experience that asked the questions boomers were asking about faith and God and Jesus. At the time, *Christianity Today* said, "Many Christians have ignored this generation's questions about Jesus. For those who will listen, *Superstar* tells what young people are saying."[28]

Two characters generated the most controversy. Mary Magdalene sang, "I Don't Know How to Love Him," which insinuated a love relationship that made conservatives uncomfortable. Judas sang "Superstar," asking Jesus why he had let things get so out of hand, which challenged the belief in a divinely inspired Jesus who had it all together.

Rice said one of the intents of the musical was "to show the way people react to him." Jesus himself was portrayed as a humanitarian thinker and the charismatic leader of a dissident movement who became a victim of his fame and power and died as a martyr for his people.

What made *Superstar* important was that it made Jesus accessible to the boomer generation. Its message was packaged in a way that boomers could relate to, and it gave them a chance to examine their beliefs in relationship to this Jesus. It scratched the core of what many boomers had been seeking, a religious experience that dug beneath the ritual and rationality of their parents' religion and challenged the technological materialism that dominated so much of their lives. Beyond the protests, the long hair, the hippie clothing, the adolescent rebellion, and the loud music was a secret desire to be godly, to be made whole, to be one with the creation, to find meaning and purpose, to belong.

Not finding what they needed in institutionalized religion, millions of boomers went on a search that led them away from Jesus and the church that proclaimed him. Many would flock to new expressions of Christianity that catered to their needs. Others went on a journey into dark and strange places and have never come back.

CHAPTER 6

Supernaturalism

In the world of the supernatural, everything is possible and nothing is unbelievable. It is a world populated by angels and devils, extraterrestrials and mystics, spirit guides and Buddha, ancient voices, and channelers. Its source of knowledge ranges from the gnostic gospels to *Siddhartha*, from Native American religions to Eastern mysticism, from astrology to the channeled teachings of the ascended masters. Its tools include Ouija boards, tarot cards, runes, crystals, I Ching, the *Tibetan Book of the Dead*, star charts, numerology, hypnosis, and the Bible. Its dialogue is filled with words like karma, the light, at-one-ment, the wave, channeling, ESP, reincarnation, cosmic energy, inner healing, holistic health, psychic ability, chakras, and the New Age.

To enter into this strange new world, you need only to be open and willing to seek the god that is within, to find the divine self, to realize that you are "God." Its basic worldview is ignored by mainline Protestants, railed at by conservative fundamentalists, and strangely enough, embraced in some ways by Pentecostals and charismatics. Like the black market in a totalitarian country, supernaturalism makes up the vast underbelly of the American religious economy. It is a world that first attracted boomers and now is seen through the pop culture of their children and grandchildren.

It's the underlying theology seen in book and film series like *Harry Potter, Twilight,* and *Star Wars*. It fuels the interest in television shows like *The Walking Dead, The Vampire Diaries,* and *True Blood*.

To understand the impact of this worldview, we first need to come to grips with what Tom Wolfe in 1982 called the Third Great Awakening—an awakening to God and to all things spiritual that broke into the collective consciousness during the formative years of the boomer generation in the late '60s and early '70s.

A good place to start is the musical *Hair*. When it came to Broadway in 1968, it scandalized theatergoers because of its nude dancing. But it enthralled boomers with its message of peace, love, and acceptance, which was a sign of the Age of Aquarius. The song from the musical made famous by the Fifth Dimension, "Let the Sunshine In"[1] became a number-one hit with its words proclaiming the "dawning" of the Age of Aquarius.

Catch words and phrases from "Let the Sunshine In," such as "harmony," "golden living dreams of visions," "mystic crystal revelations," and "love will steer the stars," captured the imagination and placed this Aquarian vision in opposition to the scientific worldview, which had given us two world wars, Vietnam, and the bomb. The musical was filled with dancing, energy, freedom, and joy. It promoted a new vision of the world where the color of one's skin did not divide and where love and peace ruled.

In many ways, the musical was the personification of the highest ideals of the counterculture, which pulled its ideas from sources outside of mainstream America and was just as comfortable talking about realigning a person's chakras as another person would be talking about the latest baseball scores. The worldview of the counterculture embraced nature and valued the stuff of this earth over the urban world of concrete and glass. It looked for spiritual enlightenment aided by marijuana and LSD. It longed for freedom of expression and embraced the most important characteristic of all, the ability to create, to add one's voice to the harmony of the universe.

This was in direct opposition to the worldview of the early twentieth century that embraced science and the creation of a secular society as the ideal for human endeavor. Whereas the spiritual world is filled with emotion and unproven insights, the scientific worldview offers an objective, rational way of developing a world that meets the needs of humanity.

The problem with this objective consciousness is that the only one who can have it is the dispassionate scientist whose goal is to be devoid of all emotions, feelings, and opinions in order to make an objective analysis of whatever he or she is studying. As a result, all of life is viewed as a grand experiment that can be measured, collated, analyzed, evaluated, surveyed, and classified.

The world is divided between the "scientist," whose chief characteristic is a hard core of rationality, and the "subjects" of scientific inquiry who have messy emotions, feelings, and, worst of all, opinions, which tend to skew the findings of the so-called experts.

In the name of scientific inquiry, soldiers were exposed to nuclear blasts to test their readiness to fight in such conditions; students were given LSD to study their reactions to this new wonder drug; healthy animals were subjected to surgeries and injections to test new methods; artificial hearts were placed into the chests of dying patients; brain cells of fetuses were scooped out and used to try to cure the diseases of elderly patients; prisoners were given any number of pharmaceutical products to see their results; and drug companies tried out new drugs in third-world countries to perfect them for the North American market.

The perfect manifestation of this objective consciousness is the creation of the machine that can process millions of bits of information in a second and can measure, tabulate, and perform skills in endless repetition with flawless objectivity. When something goes wrong, it can be fixed simply, without fuss, and you do not have to pay its Social Security. To make this great machine work, you have to regulate time into a rigid rhythm of the clock, which keeps all things tied together in perfectly measurable, controllable segments of existence. Any other experience of time is mystical or supernatural.

The biggest problem with the scientific myth is that it robs life of the experience of joy. Since everything can be measured in relationship to some kind of objective scale hatched from the brain of the objective scientist, nothing in this world is special, wondrous, or extraordinary. Even life itself has come about because of an accidental thrashing of atoms in the atmosphere. Theodore Roszak in *The Making of a Counter Culture* commented:

> Consider the strange compulsion our biologists have to synthesize life in a test tube—and the seriousness with which this project is taken. Every dumb beast of the earth knows without thinking once about it how to create life: it does so by seeking delight where it shines most brightly. But, the biologist argues, once we have done it in a laboratory, then we shall really know what it is all about. Then we shall be able to improve upon it![2]

With the supremacy of the rational, objective, scientific worldview comes the death of joy and experience. Objectivity breeds mutated personalities that can see nature only as something to be conquered, view people as things to be persuaded and surveyed, and think God is dead.

In contrast to the myth of objectivity, supernaturalism says there is a vast realm of experience that embraces all that life has to offer, that places one's heart at the disposal of the creative forces of the universe, that focuses on the making rather than on the made, and that enables a person to become a whole being filled with the totality of all the experiences and emotions that make a person human.

The Boomers' Embrace of Experience

In the late '60s and early '70s, technocracy's children shed the myth of objectivity like a snake's skin and embraced experience in all its manifestations in the world of the supernatural. They turned to the East and grappled with Buddhism. They resonated with its idea of faith not as an ideological underpinning, but as a mystic vision. Buddhism represented a tradition that taught you had to close your eyes to objective reality to perceive the wholeness and beauty of all that is. This had great appeal to a generation that felt itself drowning in a sea of words without emotional roots and personal connections.

Buddhism also gained adherents because of its teaching to become one with nature. This was in sharp contrast with traditional Western Christianity, which seemed to teach that humanity is nature's overlord. In the nineteenth and twentieth centuries, Christians exercised this lordship in a way that some thought brought ecological ruin to the world. Buddhism, on the other hand, says that we are not separate from the world but are part of it, that to find oneself, one has to be in union with all of creation.

Another core teaching of Buddhism that is in contrast to Christianity is that its sense of salvation is negative in direction. Buddhism does not aim at building the kingdom of God or moving on to perfection or maturing in Christ or redeeming a fallen world. Instead, for the Buddhist, the world is unreal and must be "let go" for a believer to find oneness with the universe.[3]

Psychiatrist David Elkind in 1971 commented on youth's desire to break free from the rationalistic conceit of the West. He commented that the youth of the 1970s were turned off by the dead symbols of institutional religion but still wished to explore spiritual matters. This search for meaningful symbols of spirituality led them to Eastern religions because they seemed to be so mysterious. This was in contrast to Western society, whose deification of reason had intellectualized religion to the point of alienating people from their feelings and inner world.[4]

Beyond Buddhism, other boomers in the late '60s and early '70s discovered religious meaning in homegrown movements such as Synanon, Aria, and Scientology, which began to take on a spiritual atmosphere. Esalen Institute, a lodge perched on a cliff overlooking the Pacific Ocean in Big Sur, California, specialized in group encounter sessions that were aimed at getting people to bare their souls and strip away their defensive façades. Psychedelic communes and new left communes took up the same method to help individuals find their true selves, the "Real Me."

Tom Wolfe says, "And what will the Real Me be like? It is at this point that the new movements tend to take on a religious or spiritual atmosphere. At one point or another they arrive at an axiom first propounded by the Gnostic Christians some eighteen hundred years ago: namely, that at the apex of every human soul there exists a spark of the light of God. . . . He who has dug himself out from under the junk heap of civilization can discover it."[5]

Other boomers sought to manipulate nature and time by use of occult practices. In the singles scene, the first question asked by a prospective suitor was, "What's your sign?" rather than "What's your name?" Astrology became the "in" thing with young and old alike. The wide appeal of astrology was soon followed by other occult practices such as tarot cards, numerology, Ouija boards, witchcraft, and Satanism.

Capitalizing on this interest was the film *The Exorcist*, which in 1973 became the top moneymaker of its time. I remember going to the movie with a group of friends from college. We stood in a line for three hours to get in. When we finally made it into the theater, we ended up in the front row.

Of course, the movie scared us to death, not because of its special effects or gory scenes, but because the story line was so believable. None of us had any problems believing that a girl could be possessed by the devil and that, in the end, the church would be ineffective in dealing with it. After all, it echoed the experience many of us had had with the occult.

After I became a Christian when I was fourteen, I went through a number of experiences not unknown to members of the boomer generation. Wanting the same powerful experience of the Holy Spirit I had felt when I became a Christian and not finding it again in my church, my friends and I went in a different direction; we discovered the Ouija board. In ninth and tenth grades, the Ouija board became my faithful companion. I took it with me on church campouts and introduced its power to my friends. We went through elaborate ceremonies of our own devising, lighting particular candles and making sure the shadow of the cross was on the board at all times to protect us from evil spirits.

At one church campout while our parents were in the main cabin, a group of us were using the board. It said that one of the girls had an evil spirit in her. In order to get rid of it, I was to do a series of incantations to take the evil spirit from her and put it into me to save her soul. Without thinking, I followed its instructions to the letter and that night I opened myself up to the influence of an evil spirit. Soon, I began having strange and violent dreams, some of which came true.

As I went through high school, I had something of a double life—the Christian who went to church and the occultist who used all sorts of paraphernalia to try to foretell the future. All through this time, my church was naively ignorant or reasonably tolerant of the whole thing. No one ever said anything was wrong with it. After all, it was just a game, wasn't it?

During my first year in college, a friend took me to his black Pentecostal congregation, where I was confronted with the enormity of what I was doing. That night, during an altar call, I went through a spiritual battle that freed me from the evil power that had been oppressing me. Later, I was told that through prayer and faith in Jesus, I needed to close the doors on my occult practices, and I was freed from the hold the occult had on me during my youth.

No words are adequate to explain how all this happened; no concepts wrap it up in a neat theological package. All I can say is that I know it happened to me. It is part of my spiritual journey; and as a result, I have no doubt about the power of God or the reality of a supernatural world beyond our understanding and easy definitions. Other boomers had similar experiences coming out from under the power of drugs, especially LSD. With these experiences in mind, the great search for God and spiritual truth led boomers in many different directions in their youth.

The Search for the Divine Spark

This search for the divine spark led boomers to follow a number of assorted gurus and religious movements during the 1970s and '80s. Maharishi Mahesh Yogi, the founder of the Transcendental Meditation Program, gained a wide following in the late '60s with his simplified and popular version of Hindu meditation, which he trademarked under the initials TM. Using the marketplace like a religious version of McDonald's, he courted celebrities such as the Beatles and Mia Farrow.

In 1971 he founded the Maharishi's International University, which is now an accredited university offering doctoral programs. Presented as a scientific means to reduce stress, increase productivity, and heighten creativity, TM was taught in some public schools until a federal court in New Jersey ruled that TM was really a religious exercise and could not be taught in its schools. Six million Americans were taught TM, and it became the most popular method of meditation that had sprung from Hindu roots.[6]

Other gurus who grabbed national headlines included Swami Muktananda, known as "Baba" to his followers, who taught yoga to such people as California Governor Jerry

Brown and singers John Denver and Diana Ross, among many others in the Hollywood set. His chief teaching was "God dwells within you as you; worship yourself."

Guru Maharaj Ji at the age of fifteen in 1973 claimed a worldwide following of six million. Prominent among his followers, who were called "premises," was Rennie Davis of the Chicago Seven. The founder of the Divine Light Mission, which had 248 centers across the United States, Ji appeared in stadiums across the country where followers fell at his feet as he dispensed "the knowledge" or "divine light."

In 1981 Bhagwan Shree Rajneesh moved his commune in Poona, India, to central Oregon where he bought sixty-four thousand acres of land and created his own community of God. Local residents were outraged when his commune members outvoted them and placed members of their group in city government. Rajneesh was often pictured driving in a new Rolls-Royce down a road lined by his adoring followers who bowed to him as he rode by. A vague image could be seen of him blessing them with a wave of his hand.

His ideal was to create a commune that would be "an experiment in spiritual communism . . . a space where we can create human beings who are not obsessed with comparison, who are not obsessed with the ego, who are not obsessed with personality." But by 1985 the commune was disbanded. Rajneesh was deported, and his followers were doing time for crimes ranging from wiretapping to attempted murder to arson to arranging sham marriages in order to circumvent immigration laws.[7]

Other groups that attracted negative publicity were Scientologists, Moonies from the Unification Church, and Hare Krishnas, who populated airports in their orange saris and clinking bells as they sought donations from weary travelers.

So prominent were these movements that parents hired deprogrammers to rescue their teenage children from such groups, and books came out describing the "brainwashing" techniques that were used to indoctrinate new devotees. A *Time* magazine article in 1977 on "Brainwashing Moonies" asked the question, "Should parents be allowed to hire strong-arm experts to abduct their own children and argue them into forsaking the religious cults they have joined?"[8]

While their parents feared these religious cults would take their children away, boomers saw something else. The appeal of these groups to boomers was that they offered a strong sense of community—a way of life separate from "corrupt" Western society, and they were led by charismatic teachers who seemed to have found enlightenment. One follower of Rajneesh, even after his commune fell apart, said, "I still see him as the wisest person I ever met."[9]

The Emergence of the New Age Movement

By the mid-1980s when many of these groups were called into question and discredited by the media, it was thought that in some way this grand search for "truth" was over—that boomers would find their way back home to mainline America or that they would give up on religion altogether. Instead of being pictured as devotees to a religious guru, they were seen as addicted to the materialism symbolized by the yuppies. But in 1987 the different segments of Buddhism, Hinduism, the occult, the science of mind, astrology, the teaching of Native American religions, and the belief in extraterrestrials all came together in something called the New Age movement.

In 1987 Jose Arguelles, a professor at Union Graduate School in Colorado, announced that August 16–17, 1987, would mark a new wave of history, the "Harmonic Convergence," a time when a correction would occur in the earth's resonance. In order for this correction to take place, 144,000 people would have to participate to send that vision spontaneously sparking through the imaginations of the majority of humanity. He declared that this was just the start, the opening event in which governments, the military, and polluting industries would be taken apart. By 2010 the earth would be purified and humanity would have found its place in the universal extraterrestrial community.[10]

On that weekend, 20,000 New Agers assembled at sacred sites across the country, from Central Park in New York City to Mount Shasta in Northern California, to provide harmony to the world. Participants charged their crystals with the energy of the rising sun, chanted "Ooom," danced and raised their hands in the air, and channeled for ancient ascended masters who told of a new era in human history. Because of a unique lineup of planets in the solar system, Arguelles had persuaded people that this was a high holy day for the world to prepare people for the coming of extraterrestrials who would bring us into the galactic community.

Dr. William Gooch of Hayden Planetarium in Manhattan affirmed the planetary lineup but believed nothing unusual was going on. Perhaps people just wanted to go back to the sixties.[11]

Although it was seen as a great grand joke in the media, later in the year *Time* came out with a cover story on the New Age movement, which talked about the growing number of people attracted to this spiritual quest for enlightenment. Here is what they said:

> All in all, the New Age does express a cloudy sort of religion, claiming vague connections with both Christianity and the major faiths of the East (New Agers like to say Jesus spent 18 years in India absorbing Hinduism and the teachings of Buddha), plus an occasional dab of pantheism and sorcery. The underlying faith is a lack of faith in the orthodoxies of rationalism, high technology, routine living, spiritual law-and-order. Somehow, the New Agers believe, there must be some secret and mysterious shortcut or alternative path to happiness and health. And nobody ever really dies.[12]

Although the number of New Agers was hard to come by, John Naisbitt and Patricia Aburdene in *Megatrends 2000* estimated that the number of New Agers ranged between ten and twenty million Americans.[13] Predominant among New Agers were boomers. Lillie Wilson, in the September 1988 issue of *American Demographics*, said: "New Agers tend to be educated, affluent, and successful people. They are hungry for something that mainstream society has not given them. They say they are looking for 'alternatives,' 'new paradigms,' 'social transformation,' 'personal wholeness,' 'enlightenment' and even 'utopia.' And they are willing to pay for it."[14]

New Age Journal, whose subscriptions increased 900 percent in the 1980s, stated in 1992 that 91 percent of its subscribers were college educated, with an average household income of nearly $42,000 and a median age of 39.5. The same profile held for listeners of New Age music, a blend of jazz and meditation music, which Suzanne Doucet in *Billboard* said is "designed to engage the right brain, which evokes intuition, imagination, and altered states of consciousness."[15]

Numbers do not tell the whole story because New Agers had influence beyond their population. Russell Chandler, a religion writer and award-winning journalist for the *Los Angeles Times* for eighteen years, wrote in his book *Understanding the New Age:*

> New Age influence has indeed touched every facet of contemporary life. Its popularizers and their beliefs are often visible on your television set, at the movies, in printed horoscopes, or at your local health food store. Even sports and exercise programs, motivational training, psychological counseling, and religious classes are frequent pipelines for New Age thinking.[16]

Although the name New Age is no longer used, its influence is readily seen today. Some of the founders of our most important brands like Apple and Whole Foods resonated with its values.

Oprah Winfrey's network (OWN) has broadcast a block of programing since 2011 called *Supersoul Sunday.* A description of one episode called "10 Prayers That Will Get You Through" captures the eclectic nature of this worldview. "They are the words we turn to when life presents us with unwelcome obstacles to overcome. Iyanla Vanzant, Brené Brown, Deepak Chopra and other spiritual champions share affirmations that could help you clear those hurdles."[17] Her recent series "Belief" explored all the major religious traditions with an eye to discovering the truths we can gain from each one. Underlying the series is another tenet of the New Age movement: no one faith tradition has the answer. People must discover the truth for themselves.

Anyone who does yoga, who meditates, who only buys organic food, or who recycles can credit the early pioneers of the New Age movement who wanted to get back in touch with the energy of the earth and to avail themselves of the spiritual practices of Eastern religions.

The Boomer Church

The desire that New Agers expressed for a spiritual experience was also echoed in a phenomenon that changed the way boomers did church. As boomers became young adults in the 1980s, Christian boomers were not interested in doing church the way their parents did. Many had little interest in becoming members or attending meetings or being part of faith communities where they had little say in the decision-making process.

Perhaps most frustrating to the young adults in the 1980s was most existing congregations' refusal to embrace the use of contemporary Christian music in worship. Entrenched leaders in churches saw drums, guitars, and synthesizers as representing the counterculture and rock 'n' roll, something they had tried to get their children to resist. Rather than including this new style of music—written by musicians like Amy Grant, Michael W. Smith, and Andraé Crouch—in worship, the vast majority of churches resisted change and insisted that the only appropriate music in worship were hymns and classical music. The only appropriate instruments were the organ and the piano. As a result, boomers found themselves in the midst of the worship wars of the 1980s and 1990s. Rather than fight their parents' generation, they left.

Seen from the hindsight of today, these issues may seem laughable to some; but in the 1980s and 1990s, they killed off the passion of many younger boomer pastors and drove off the sons and daughters of church members. The boomers found churches that perfectly understood what young-adult boomers who were establishing their own families were looking for—the emerging independent churches led by dynamic boomer pastors who understood their music and created what we now call the megachurch movement.

In the late 1980s, I became exposed to this emerging movement when a friend invited me to join him at the Robert H. Schuller Institute for Successful Church Leadership, an annual event held at the Crystal Cathedral in Southern California. Started in 1969, by the 1980s, the institute was the most influential training event offered to young boomer pastors and leaders who were starting their ministries. Today, there are vast numbers of large churches that offer such training, but Schuller was the first to understand the importance of teaching a curriculum beyond what pastors had learned in seminary—how to build and run a growing church.

Heavily attended by evangelical pastors from a wide variety of denominations, the Schuller Institute for Successful Church Leadership offered a new model for pastoral leadership—the pastor as entrepreneur.

This was in sharp contrast to the models taught in most seminaries—the pastor as counselor, spiritual guide, or social change agent. Schuller's nonconformist approach appealed to boomers. Schuller used nontraditional settings for worship. He started with a drive-in theater. He focused on developing a church that reached people who didn't go to church. Instead of touting his denominational affiliation, he called his church a *community church*. Instead of preaching a sermon, he gave a message. He also became the most noted preacher in the country through his weekly broadcast of the *Hour of Power*, during which he regularly included an interview with leaders in business, the arts, and sports.

Schuller also offered a blueprint for success. First, quality is key. To compete with the culture at large, everything must be first class—from the music to the child care to the worship format to the seating in the sanctuary, every effort must be made to make it the best expression of your faith.

Second, be positive. No one wants to come to church and leave feeling worse than when they arrived. Give a message that uplifts and offers people practical ways to apply their faith to daily living.

Third, don't be afraid to ask people to do their best. Rather than being ashamed to ask for financial support, remind people that the best thing they will ever do beyond raising a family is to build a church that honors God.

Fourth, develop leaders. If you have something you have learned, share it with others. If you expect to grow a congregation, develop leaders who will be able to lead its various ministries. A single person can only do so much. A team can do the impossible.

Fifth, find a need and fill it. To attract people to your church, you must first listen to them by going out into the community to ascertain their needs. Once you find out their longings, develop ministries that meet what they are looking for.

Schuller's teachings were embraced and implemented as boomer pastors launched and rebuilt moribund churches across the country. Prominent among these pastors were Bill Hybels, founder of Willow Creek Community Church outside Chicago, and Rick Warren, founder of Saddleback Valley Community Church in Orange County, California.

In 1975 Bill Hybels and his team did a community survey to discover what people were saying about churches. The biggest complaint people had with the church was that "the church is always pleading for my money."

Based on their survey, Hybels started Willow Creek using a unique approach. On Sundays, he offered a "seeker service" using drama, music, and relevant Bible-based messages for seekers who did not have to say anything, sing anything, sign anything, or give anything.

These worship services are what he called "Christianity 101 and 201." On Wednesday evenings, the church offered another worship service called "New Community," which was for born-again Christians. He called this service "Christianity 301 and 401." Much like the traditional churches of the time, it offered corporate worship and meatier teaching to challenge believers to grow in their faith in Jesus Christ.[18]

Like Schuller, Hybels put a lot of emphasis on leadership and helping Christian believers find their ministry. His leaders focused on helping new believers discover their spiritual gifts and spiritual passions.

Then the leaders at Willow Creek did something that truly set them apart from other churches of the time: they used a tool from the secular world, the Myers-Briggs personality test to encourage believers to discover their personality type.[19]

This willingness to go outside the Christian circle of knowledge and tap truth from whatever source gave Willow Creek relevance to boomers who had gone to college, had worked in the business world, and had been exposed to a wide variety of spiritual experiences. Willow Creek's seeker services had no problem playing songs off the radio or showing video clips from the latest movies as a way to connect to boomers. Here was a church that was not afraid to learn from a wide variety of sources and that could filter the information through a Christian lens in a way that made the message of the gospel relevant.

As the church grew, so did its influence. In 1995, it made one of its most significant decisions. It launched the Global Summit, a yearly two-day experience that brings together the best leaders from the church and business worlds to teach its audience the latest principles of leadership. By 2015, it was live streaming the event to more than 170,000 participants in churches around the world.[20]

Over the years, the Global Summit has included Patrick Lencioni, author of *Five Dysfunctions of a Team*; Jim Collins, author of *Good to Great*; Michelle Rhee, founder of StudentsFirst; and Jack Welch, former CEO of General Electric. Through its influence, it has had an impact on the worship styles, preaching, and evangelism strategies of churches throughout the world.

Like Hybels, Rick Warren started his church—the Saddleback Valley Community Church—after knocking on some five hundred doors in the community and asking residents what they wanted in a church. Four complaints about church kept recurring in his survey: one, sermons are boring, not relevant; two, members are unfriendly to visitors; three, most churches are more interested in your money than in you as a person; and four, quality child care is a necessity.

When he launched his first worship service, Warren sent a mailing to the community with an opening sentence that said it all: "At last! A new church for those who've given up on traditional church services."[21]

Later Warren would write two best-selling books, *The Purpose Driven Church* in 1995 and *The Purpose Driven Life* in 2002. As a member of the boomer generation, he captured boomers' desire to be difference makers. Like Hybels, he presented his ideas in a way that allowed boomers to learn from a wide variety of sources.

The Purpose Driven Life: What on Earth Am I Here For? was perfectly designed for boomers looking for a deeper spiritual experience. Rather than a typical self-help book, it was designed as a forty-day spiritual journey, with a chapter to be read each day. The first chapter starts with these words: "It's not about you. The purpose of your life is far greater than your own personal fulfillment, your peace of mind, or even your happiness. It's far greater than your family, your career, and even your wildest dreams and ambitions. If you want to know why you were placed on this planet, you must begin with God. You were born *by* his purpose and *for* his purpose."[22]

Boomers and the Megachurch Boom

Willow Creek and Saddleback were on the forefront of a new wave of churches started by boomers that have come to dominate the Christian religious scene. The model of the pastor as entrepreneur provided a new template for developing large churches with more than 2,000 in attendance.

In 1970, there were fifty churches with more than 2,000 in worship on a weekend. By 2010, more than 1,600 churches with more than six million participants gathered for worship on a weekend. This is twice as much as the more than 32,000 United Methodist churches in the United States had in 2014, with slightly fewer than three million on a weekend.[23] Forty percent of megachurches are nondenominational, 16 percent are Southern Baptists, and only 2 percent are United Methodists, with no other mainline churches on the list.[24]

Of course, the history of megachurches is not without its problems. Schuller's Crystal Cathedral fell apart after his family could not come up with a plan for who would succeed him. The property was bought by the Roman Catholic Church and is now a center for worship and ministry for Catholics in Orange Country. Some high-power churches like Mars Hill in Seattle dissolved after scandals rocked the leadership of the 13,000-member church. Many of those churches that were started by

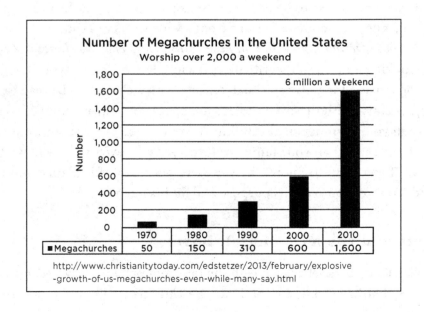

Number of Megachurches in the United States
Worship over 2,000 a weekend

	1970	1980	1990	2000	2010
■ Megachurches	50	150	310	600	1,600

http://www.christianitytoday.com/edstetzer/2013/february/explosive-growth-of-us-megachurches-even-while-many-say.html boomers are facing the challenge of succession: How does the ministry continue when the founder retires?

Willow Creek also hit a bump in the road when a survey of its congregation in 2004 discovered that 25 percent of the people in the church were stalled in their spirituality or dissatisfied and thinking of leaving the church. At first glance, this sounded like Willow Creek had failed in the most elemental aspect of church life, but a closer look at the research unveils deeper insights that apply to churches of all sizes.[25]

Willow Creek's leaders discovered that church participation did not automatically equate with a deeper faith journey. Active participation in a faith community was important for people who were new to the Christian faith or were new to a particular church, but going to church did not mean growth in their love of God. In fact, as people grew closer to God through personal prayer, reading the Bible, and solitude, the church became less important for their spiritual growth.

The church's leaders discovered something else: the goal of churches should not be to make people better churchgoers. The goal should be to teach people to develop their personal spiritual disciplines so they can grow in their relationship to Jesus.[26]

They also found many spiritually mature Christians had become dissatisfied because the church was so focused on newcomers that they felt they were not being helped to grow deeper. Rather than cast them off, Willow Creek realized these dissatisfied Christians were critical to their ability to share the Christian faith with new people and were the key contributors to the overall life of the congregation.

The Role of Boomer Pastors

In churches across the country, boomers have aged into responsibility and are now the leaders. In The United Methodist Church, this leadership is clearly seen in the age of its clergy in full connection—elders. In 1985, 27 percent of elders were fifty-five to seventy-two years of age. In 2015, 55 percent of elders were age fifty-five to seventy-two. Conversely, in 1985, 15 percent of elders were under the age of thirty-five; and by 2015, this number had shrunk to 7 percent.

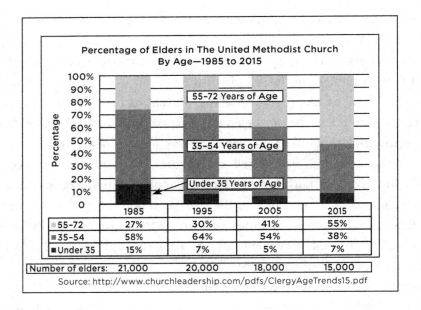

Percentage of Elders in The United Methodist Church By Age—1985 to 2015			
	1985	1995	2005	2015
55–72	27%	30%	41%	55%
35–54	58%	64%	54%	38%
Under 35	15%	7%	5%	7%
Number of elders:	21,000	20,000	18,000	15,000

Source: http://www.churchleadership.com/pdfs/ClergyAgeTrends15.pdf

Similar numbers are seen for deacons at 49 percent and local pastors at 55 percent. According to the *Lewis Center Report on Clergy Age Trends in the United Methodist Church,* what was true for Methodists was also true for other mainline denominations. Most had more than 50 percent of their clergy over the age of fifty-five.[27]

By 2025, most of these boomer pastoral leaders will be retired, and churches will be challenged to fill the leadership gap. Much of what happens to the wider church will depend on the boomer pastors themselves and how they view their last official years as pastoral leaders. While they will need to set the stage for the next generation of leaders, they also have the task of preparing their fellow boomer congregants for the second half of life. Boomers will look for churches that take seriously their desire for a deeper spirituality that will allow them to grow in their love of Jesus.

As boomers move deeper into the second half of life, churches of all sizes will have a second chance to connect with them. Once they become empty nesters or retire from work, their whole value system will be up for grabs. For boomers, the ongoing questions of meaning and purpose are not going away. In fact, as they age, these questions will only intensify as they look to answer two additional questions that will fuel their spiritual quest: "What am I going to leave behind? What is my legacy?"

As boomers age, they will have an opportunity to explore their faith, to learn how to pray deeply, to have time to be connected to others in small groups, to share their faith with their children and grandchildren, and to be in service to others in the community. The question for the church is whether it will be there for the boomers as they pursue God. For regardless of what the church does, boomers will continue the journey they started when they were young.

The desire for spiritual experience that permeated their youth continues to have an impact in the lives of boomers today. As a generation, boomers hold to the notion that there is more to this life than meets the eye, that beyond this earth is a spiritual world of which they can avail themselves to find meaning and purpose and, more than meaning, a personal experience of salvation.

CHAPTER
7

Wholeness

Every day until 2034, ten thousand boomers in the United States will be moving beyond sixty years of age. As a group, they will be facing the opportunities of living an extended life in numbers that have never been seen before. Beyond the United States, the growth of an aging population is one of the greatest challenges facing the world as it grapples with providing the resources needed to care for a maturing population.

Worldwide, the number of those who are over sixty will grow from 901 million in 2015 to over 2 billion by 2050. The worldwide growth of this group will go from 12.3 percent of the total population in 2015 to 21.5 percent in 2050. These demographic changes will have the most profound effect in developing countries, which—according to the Global Age Watch organization—will be home to eight out of ten of the world's over-sixty population.[1]

In the United States, the number of people over age sixty will grow from 20.7 percent to 27.9 percent of the population; whereas, in Japan it will go from 33.1 percent to 42.5 percent. One of the reasons China just reversed its one-child policy to allow couples to have two children is that China sees a future where 36.5 percent of the population will be over sixty by 2050.[2]

This titanic shift in population will affect every policy decision, every budget consideration, and every choice that governments at all levels will make. Housing, medical

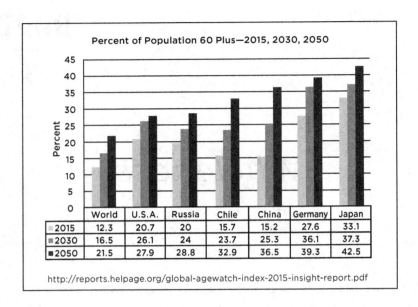

Percent of Population 60 Plus—2015, 2030, 2050

	World	U.S.A.	Russia	Chile	China	Germany	Japan
2015	12.3	20.7	20	15.7	15.2	27.6	33.1
2030	16.5	26.1	24	23.7	25.3	36.1	37.3
2050	21.5	27.9	28.8	32.9	36.5	39.3	42.5

http://reports.helpage.org/global-agewatch-index-2015-insight-report.pdf

care, transportation, food, education, religious practices, family life, and entertainment will be touched and, in some cases, transformed by a robust and vocal aging population.

As the boomer generation in the United States ages, its members will have a chance to reinvent themselves and to do the things they always wanted to do. Some will retire like their parents did in a retirement complex that caters to all their needs. Others will travel to see the world. Most will look for part-time work to supplement their benefits. Others will look for ways to give back by volunteering in nonprofit organizations in their communities. Many will relish the role of grandparent and will help with child care as needed. Some will raise their grandchildren as if they were their own.

As we have seen, the values of brokenness, loneliness, rootlessness, and self-seeking defined the boomers' experience of growing up. What is less obvious is that these core values still influence their worldview. Once individual boomers leave the workforce and move into the next phase of life, these people will have plenty of time on their hands. As they live into the future, these boomers will see the values of brokenness, loneliness, rootlessness, and self-seeking reassert themselves as the boomers move further into the second half of life.

Beyond these core values, godliness and supernaturalism capture boomers' need for meaning and purpose. Churches and other groups that wish to connect with this generation must also be aware of another profound value that resonates deep in the soul of boomers—the desire for wholeness.

As boomers age, they will want to make the circle of faith, work, family, and leisure into a complete package that will enable them to make sense of their lives. The material goods they have collected will become less important; instead, a focus on well-being, family ties, friendships, and spirituality will occupy their lives.

A report from Nielson and Boomagers on "Boomers: Marketing's Most Valuable Generation" says the following,

> For the Boomers, the notion of retirement has all but disappeared. While aging is inevitable and irreversible, Boomers are rethinking this phase of life just as they have redefined all of the other conventions of their lifestyle along the way. They are emboldened by a sense of agelessness, and they plan to continue to lead their lives as they always have. They do not see these as years of retirement; instead, they see them as their encore years. They are still playing, and they are saving their best performance for last.[3]

This desire for wholeness will be played out in the following five trends: (1) health span more important than life span; (2) the generational racial and ethnic divide; (3) facing mortality; (4) the future of faith; and (5) the pursuit of wholeness. Some of these trends will help boomers find what they are looking for. Some are obstacles that will hinder them. Each of these trends provides opportunities to enhance the lives of boomers in their second half of life.

Health Span More Important Than Life Span

Nothing quite captures the boomers' quest for happiness and self-fulfillment than the commercials aired during the thirty-minute national news on ABC, CBS, and NBC. Knowing that younger generations get their news from Twitter and Facebook, advertisers are confident that the predominant audience of the thirty-minute nightly news programs are boomers and members of older generations who still remember getting their news from Walter Cronkite, Dan Rather, and Peter Jennings.

Almost every commercial shows healthy, vibrant fifty- and sixty-year-olds walking on a beach, hiking in a meadow with a majestic mountain in the background, or sitting at a table eating an organic meal. But what is most important, they are holding hands with someone, sitting in bathtubs, or hanging out with a group of friends—and they are smiling and laughing.

What is bringing them such joy? A wide variety of drugs guaranteed to cure their various illnesses: Crestor for high-blood pressure, Porlia to strengthen bones, Humira for arthritis, Lyrica for nerve damage, and Viagra for erectile dysfunction.

The commercials always begin with a message about the positive effects of the drug. While boomers are having a party on the screen, the commercials delineate the side effects—increased risk of heart attack, a puffy face, or a desire to kill oneself. The hope of the drug companies is that the images of happiness will overcome any concerns about the side effects, the idea being that the side effect will only affect other people, not the individual watching the commercials.

These commercials highlight a major issue boomers are concerned about as they age. As people move beyond sixty, the issue of how old you are is replaced by how well you are. Depending on one's health, an eighty-year-old who is fit could have a more active life than a sixty-year-old who is beset by debilitating illnesses.

Bill Gifford, in his book *Spring Chicken: Stay Young Forever (Or Die Trying)*, tells the story of two brothers, his grandfather, Leonard, and great-uncle, Emerson. As a boy, Gifford remembered going to his grandfather's birthday celebration. While his grandfather was swimming in the lake, Emerson, who was just eighteen months older than his brother, was huddled on a rocker on the porch barely communicating with those around him.

What was the difference? Leonard had been an active person all his life and enjoyed his daily work in his garden. He ate well and had given up smoking a long time ago, in contrast to his brother who still smoked and refused to go to the doctor. As Emerson aged, he was beset with one illness after another, while Leonard had an active life. Gifford says, "The result was he [my grandfather] enjoyed a longer life—and a much longer healthy life—than his brother. Public-health experts now call this *healthspan*, one's span of healthy years."[4]

If you think about it, what we hope for is not just to live to a ripe old age. What we want is a longer health span. We want to be engaged in the issues of the day, to be connected to other people, and to be able to physically do the things we want to do for as long as we can.

This is more than just living. Having a longer health span means a person has additional time to invest in others, to contribute to his or her family, and to be an active participant in a wide range of experiences.

Just as boomers cornered the market on hula hoops when they were kids, they will flood the market with the demand for drugs, antiaging treatments, and diet plans. It wasn't by happenstance that Oprah bought 10 percent of Weight Watchers and joined its board of directors. She knows that a financial stake in Weight Watchers will give her a financial windfall down the line, because so many fellow boomers want to get healthy by losing weight.[5]

In the future, more adult diapers will be sold than baby diapers. New surgical procedures for knee replacements, hip replacements, and rotator cuff repairs will speed recovery, drive down costs, and make them more accessible for a wider number of people. As technology advances, genetic testing will customize treatments for cancer and other debilitating diseases like arthritis and Parkinson's disease.

Many boomers are not waiting to get sick. They have decided to take ownership of their health and focus on prevention and fitness. The International Health Racquet and Sportsclub Association reports that its fastest growing clientele are those fifty-five and above.[6] In 1990, this group had 1.9 million health club members. In 2014, it had grown 532 percent to 12 million members.

Physically fit boomers are swelling the ranks of marathoners, triathletes, and competitors in the Senior Olympics. There is one humorous story of a *New York Times* columnist who, as a serious boomer marathoner, complained about the twentysomething "slackers" who were ruining races. What was the problem? They were running too slowly.[7]

Organizations that want to connect with boomers need to pay attention to this desire for a longer health span. Weeklong experiences that focus on creating a healthy diet and developing a workout regime are very popular. Classes that teach healthy cooking, walking clubs, and using a church gym for exercise are ways to facilitate boomers' desire to create healthy lifestyles for themselves and their families. Small groups that focus on creating a healthy lifestyle that integrates spiritual life will be in demand.

In 2013, Rick Warren, the founder of one of the largest boomer churches in the country, Saddleback Valley Community Church, and author of the best-selling *Purpose-Driven Life*, came out with another book that perfectly fits this boomer desire for a longer health span. *The Daniel Plan* is a forty-day diet and fitness plan designed to get boomers in shape. The book is built on the premise that your spirituality, emotional well-being, relationships, and ability to do productive work are based on one basic thing—your physical life. When the book was released, it was a *New York Times* best seller, and thousands of churches around the country have used it as a resource to help people in their congregations live into a longer health span.

Maintaining one's health and having as long a health span as is possible is a top priority for the boomer generation. For some, being healthy means they will have a more enjoyable life. For others, it's a matter of survival. If they can't stay healthy, they can't work. If they can't work, their whole way of life is at risk.

The Generational Racial and Ethnic Divide

Even though I live in Nashville, I spend at least a couple of weeks each year in Southern California visiting my family and my wife's family. I was born and raised in California. My Euro-American roots extend to Ireland on my father's side to a great-something grandfather who arrived in the colonies before the Revolutionary War. On my mom's side, I remember my Norwegian grandfather who immigrated to the United States when he was twenty years old. He married my Swedish grandmother, who also came to the United States during the great European immigrant wave of the early 1900s.

My wife's family also lives in the L.A. area. She was born in China, raised in Hong Kong, and came to the United States with her brothers and sister when she was a teenager.

Our visits in the Los Angeles area are always a whirlwind of activity. Part of the time is spent in the midst of the Chinese immigrant community and the other is spent in the midst of the Euro-American California culture. Although these two communities share the same 626 area code, they are worlds apart.

When I am with my wife's family, we frequent the many Asian restaurants and businesses that populate the San Gabriel Valley. One of our favorite complexes has a huge restaurant that seats hundreds of people for their famous dim sum, as servers with carts bring a wide variety of choices to the table. Har gau, sui mai, and char siu bao are among our favorites. Next door is the 99 Ranch Market, a store in the popular Chinese supermarket chain that specializes in food products from Asia. After getting our groceries, we often go next door to enjoy the favorite drink of the Chinese American young, boba tea.

When I am there, I am typically the only Euro-American in the area. I doubt my side of the family even knows these places exist, even though it's fewer than five miles away from their home.

When I am with my sister's family, we have to make sure to go to In-N-Out Burger, a famous California burger joint. We go to Red Lobster for shrimp and Marie Callender's for their soup, cornbread, and pie. We pick up groceries at Ralphs, a national supermarket chain owned by Kroger, that sells basic goods like milk and flour, organic food, and hot take-out meals. If we need a caffeine blast, we know that Starbucks is just a few minutes away.

My family experience is a small window into the new cultural divide that is seen not only in California, but in places throughout the country that have experienced the growth of immigration from Asia, Mexico, and Latin America.

White Boomers in the Midst of a Multiethnic World

By 2030, the youngest population, those seventeen and younger, in the United States will have reached minority-majority status, with 54 percent of their population having a heritage that is Asian, Hispanic, Black, Pacific Islander, Native American, or those who identify as two or more races. This youngest generation will primarily be the American-born children, grandchildren, or great-grandchildren of their first-generation ancestors.

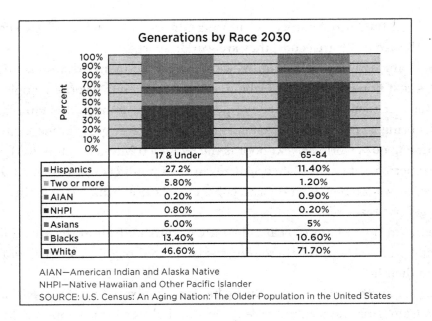

	17 & Under	65-84
■ Hispanics	27.2%	11.40%
■ Two or more	5.80%	1.20%
■ AIAN	0.20%	0.90%
■ NHPI	0.80%	0.20%
■ Asians	6.00%	5%
■ Blacks	13.40%	10.60%
■ White	46.60%	71.70%

AIAN—American Indian and Alaska Native
NHPI—Native Hawaiian and Other Pacific Islander
SOURCE: U.S. Census: An Aging Nation: The Older Population in the United States

In contrast, 71 percent of boomers, who will be ages sixty-six to eighty-four in 2030, will be white. This remarkable racial-ethnic gap is filled with implications, about which another book could be written. But here are a couple of thoughts regarding this demographic reality.[8]

As the younger, more diverse population finds its voice, it will challenge the older, majority white boomers over a number of issues. This is already being seen on college campuses where older, primarily white administrators are under increased pressure by their students to put more money into hiring professors who represent the growing racial and ethnic diversity of the student body, to setting up black, Asian, and Latino study programs, and to offering more scholarships for black and Latino students.

Some of our most prominent tech companies such as Apple, Google, and Facebook have been challenged by their lack of diversity. Even the most popular of awards shows, the Oscars, has been embroiled in controversy by presenting a slate of nominees that was all white.

Movements like Black Lives Matter challenge older Americans, especially white Americans, to confront institutional racism that keeps younger black people from the American dream. Videos of unarmed young black men shot by police bring into focus a justice system that is desperately in need of reform and seems hell-bent on killing or imprisoning young black men. Protests by athletes who refuse to stand during the playing of the national anthem provoke conversations about what it means to be an American.

Some of the most-heated exchanges in the 2016 presidential debates were between two white first-wave boomers, both of whom tried to prove that the other candidate was the most racist. Clinton and Trump both went to great lengths to prove they were free of any taint of prejudice in an attempt to woo younger multiethnic voters.

By 2030, when the vast majority of boomers will be out of the workforce and dependent on government programs like Social Security and Medicare, it will be the younger, more diverse population that will decide how to fund these programs that benefit boomers, while at the same time trying to figure out how to pay for the care of their children. Beyond the issues related to economics, the question of race and cultural differences between the generations will have a part to play in the decisions that are made.

The Challenge for Immigrant First-Generation Boomers

But it's not just white boomers who will be challenged by the diversity of the younger generations. Boomers who were born outside the United States also find themselves in a cultural divide with their children and grandchildren who were born in the United States. In California and other states with high immigration, the number of immigrant boomers is almost equal to the number of white boomers who live in the area. Their culture, language, and identity are closely tied to their national roots. But their children and grandchildren were born in the United States. In fact, about 25 percent of the children in the United States today have at least one parent born outside the United States.[9]

Like the white and black American-born members of the boomer generation, first-generation immigrants tend to live comfortably in their own language and cultural groups, while their children's and grandchildren's generations live in a culturally diverse group that is defining an updated image of what it means to be an American.

While the identity of second- and third-generation Americans is influenced by the heritage of their first-generation parents and grandparents, their culture is American. Their native language is English. As a result, boomer immigrants are experiencing a generation gap with their children and grandchildren, as their offspring identify much more closely with the American culture than with the culture of their parents' or grandparents' homelands.

In addition, most church ministries that have been successful with Hispanics, Latinos, and Asians have been developed on a model that revolves around the needs of the first generation, with worship being offered in their native languages. But because their children and grandchildren are being raised in a multicultural and multiethnic world, churches will need to develop new approaches to create meaningful connections with the younger population.

In the article "Not Your Grandmother's Little Saigon," the *Los Angeles Times* highlights the story of the transformation of the area of Orange County, CA, known as Little Saigon. It was the destination point for Vietnamese refugees after the fall of Vietnam in the 1970s. Once a safe enclave for Vietnamese immigrants, it has become a vibrant community where a mix of businesses catering to many different cultures is giving it new life.

Tim Hoang of Huntington Beach said he did not like coming to Little Saigon with his parents when he was growing up in the 1980s. But his children "actually ask to be taken to Little Saigon, where you can hear four or five languages spoken inside one business, and where we had a meal while listening to rap on the radio. Imagine that—rap."[10]

Black Boomers and the Post-Civil Rights Generation

Jasmine Rose Smothers and F. Douglas Powe Jr. explore similar issues within the African American community and in black churches in their book *Not Safe for Church: Ten Commandments for Reaching New Generations*. They focus on the cultural divide between the civil rights generation and the post-civil rights generations born after 1961 and note three things that keep the older generation from accepting the younger, post-civil rights generation: First, they are afraid of the younger generation and wonder if they let in people with tattoos and a different dress code, will they be safe in their own churches. Second, they fear too many changes in worship styles and music will make the church unfamiliar and they will lose their church home. Third, some remember times when they tried new things that didn't work. As a result, the generation born before 1961 finds itself unable or unwilling to make the connections that will allow it to share faith with the younger generations.[11]

Smothers and Powe say, "Many churches feel like they are in a tug-of-war with the post-civil rights generations and unchurched individuals. Those in the church are entrenched and ready for battle, but their opponents are not engaged in the struggle. In part, this is because the struggle is about saving the church, which is not a fight many outside of the church are interested in participating in. What is at stake for those inside the congregation is very different from those on the other end of the rope."[12]

This quote brings to forefront a thought that is almost inconceivable for boomers, especially for those whose lives revolve around their faith and places of worship—the younger the population, the less interested they are in being part of a church.

Demographic Change Challenges Mainline Churches

For churches, especially mainline churches like The United Methodist Church, these demographic shifts present a great challenge. In 2015, 89 percent of the membership of The United Methodist Church was white, and the average age was fifty-seven.[13]

Across the American landscape in rural, suburban, and urban areas, there are countless churches whose membership is one race or ethnicity and whose community is multiethnic. As the older membership struggles to find new members and keep the doors open, the wider community only knows the churches as buildings on a street. As denominational offices struggle with what to do with churches that are caught in a time warp of the past, communities are undergoing rapid change as they gentrify, look for ways to unlock gridlock, and are confronted with the growing inequality between the rich and the poor.

Churches that will thrive in the future will be closely tied to their ability to attract and keep younger generations who live in a vastly different cultural landscape than older, primarily monocultural faith communities. In addition, churches that are geared to connecting with first-generation immigrants will also be faced with the challenge of how they create ministries for their English-speaking children and grandchildren.

The Questions Around Race Will Remain at the Forefront

In the wider culture, the questions of race, privilege, and immigration will remain at the forefront. For boomers, diversity is something that is kept at a comfortable distance. It's something that feels right, but is hard to live out. They address it by attending diversity workshops or having special days for particular racial groups. The goal is accepting other cultures, learning from them, and tolerating their differences. In contrast, for the youngest generations, diversity is a way of life. It is who they are. It is their culture.

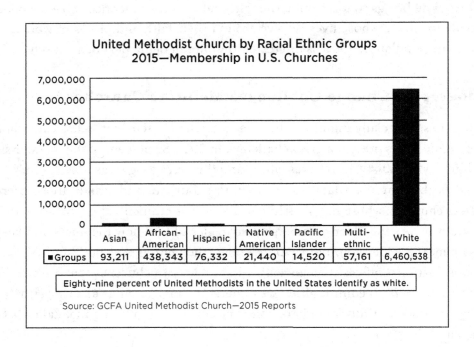

United Methodist Church by Racial Ethnic Groups
2015—Membership in U.S. Churches

	Asian	African-American	Hispanic	Native American	Pacific Islander	Multi-ethnic	White
■Groups	93,211	438,343	76,332	21,440	14,520	57,161	6,460,538

Eighty-nine percent of United Methodists in the United States identify as white.

Source: GCFA United Methodist Church—2015 Reports

In the future, boomers will find themselves part of a national discourse on who benefits from which government policies, who will pay for the needs of an aging population, how will economic and political power be passed to a much more diverse younger population, and who will take care of the young. The future of all the generations will depend on boomers' ability and willingness to be part of a conversation about issues that are painful, hurtful, and filled with landmines.

As the baton of leadership in the workplace, in government, in schools, and in the church is passed to the next generation, boomers will play a key role. Will they fight change with all their being? Will they mentor new leaders, even if they have a different heritage from themselves? Will they listen and learn from their younger colleagues? Or will they bite their tongues until they retire and be glad it is over?

Facing Mortality

When it comes to life and death, there seems to be no rhyme or reason as to who will live a long life and whose life will be cut short. Michael Jackson, Whitney Houston, Steve Jobs, Patrick Swayze, Robin Williams, Prince, and Carrie Fisher are boomers who died way too early in life.

The one truth that cannot be avoided is that death awaits us all. For boomers and society as a whole, this presents a problem. There are not enough long-term care centers, rest homes, hospice-care facilities, or plots in graveyards to handle the tremendous burden the large number of boomers will place on the health-care system and the funeral business.

Just finding a doctor could be a problem in the future. The Association of American Medical Colleges (AAMC) predicts a shortfall of 46,000 doctors by 2025. This number could increase to 90,000, depending on how many boomer doctors retire, how many medical practices will use nurse practitioners as the first line of treatment, and how many retailers like CVS and Walgreens set up clinics that offer basic treatments for colds, eye infections, and sprained ankles.[14]

Darrell G. Kirch, AAMC's chief executive, says, "An increasingly older, sicker population, as well as people living longer with chronic diseases, such as cancer, is the reason for the increased demand."[15]

The biggest need is for doctors who will focus on treatment for diseases of old age. More surgeons will be needed to treat cancer and heart problems. Others will be needed to fix and mend the broken hips, damaged knees, and torn rotator cuffs that come with aging.

Perhaps the most troubling is the growing awareness that as boomers are improving their overall health and living longer, more people will be susceptible to Alzheimer's disease and dementia.

According to the Alzheimer's Association, more than 5 million people over the age of sixty-five had Alzheimer's or dementia in 2015. This number will increase almost threefold to 13.8 million in 2050. Costs will skyrocket from $226 billion to over $1.1 trillion.[16]

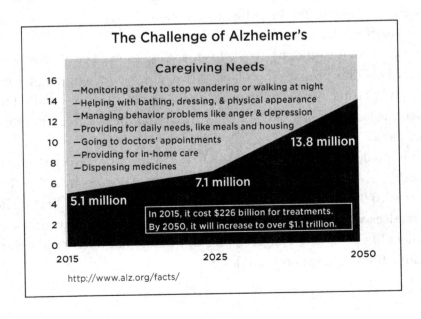

The Burden of Caregiving

The first line of care for Alzheimer's and dementia is the family. Spouses, siblings, children, grandchildren, nieces, nephews, and other relatives make up the potential pool of caregivers for the person affected. Alzheimer's and dementia are progressive diseases with no known cure, so the length of caregiving can be as long as twenty years.

Boomers are well aware of the issues involved, as many of them are now tasked with taking care of a parent who is affected by these brain diseases. My mom, who is in her nineties, lives with my sister, who is now my mother's primary caregiver. Because dementia affects the brain, life with a person with dementia is full of surprises. Many times, my mom will wake up in the middle of the night and get fully dressed, thinking it's time to go out. Or she will be found having a conversation with a group of friends when there is no one in the room. Then there was the time she sneaked out of the house without her cane or her shoes and walked about a mile to the local grocery store.

Caregivers find themselves in a weird mix of emotions, especially when the caregiver is a child now taking care of a parent. Memories both positive and negative can come into play. All kinds of questions arise. What is the best way to keep my parent safe while respecting his or her privacy? When do I know when it's too much for me to handle? What kind of help can I get? How am I going to pay for this? Should I feel guilty if I want a break? How much longer can I do this? Is it time for a care facility? Will she hate me if I send her there?

Multiply this, and you will begin to understand the impact that caregiving is having on millions of boomer families. Now, jump into the future, when the boomers themselves will need caregivers; and you will discover a painful reality. The number of front-line caregivers, those family members who are willing to take on the responsibility for caring for older family members, is dwindling.

A report from AARP says the number of potential family caregivers per person over eighty will go from 7.9 people in 2010, to 4.1 people in 2025, to 2.9 in 2050.[17] As a result, there will be an increased burden on government, community, and health services to take care of the boomers affected by dementia and a host of other diseases and injuries when they are old. But for some, these issues are hitting now.

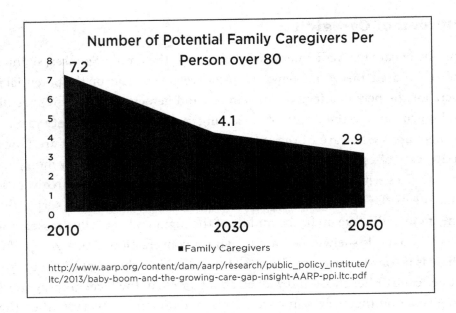

Number of Potential Family Caregivers Per Person over 80

7.2 — 4.1 — 2.9

2010 — 2030 — 2050

■ Family Caregivers

http://www.aarp.org/content/dam/aarp/research/public_policy_institute/
ltc/2013/baby-boom-and-the-growing-care-gap-insight-AARP-ppi.ltc.pdf

An article in the *Huffington Post* tells the sad story of Judith Cummings, a successful investment banker who ran triathlons and remained single all her life. Her life was dedicated to her work, and she cherished her solitude in the midst of the hectic lifestyle she led in the business world.

At age sixty-nine, she was living in a rest home in an advanced stage of dementia. As she had no family or friends, she was totally dependent on the staff. With no one to be her advocate or to support her in her treatment, it was up to her doctor and her nurses to decide the best path of treatment as she suffered from the debilitating effects of her disease.[18]

This story brings up an uncomfortable fact of life when it comes to the boomer generation: with the high number of divorces and boomers living alone, almost one-third will not have the family support network that their parents' generation enjoyed.

To fill the caregiving gap, the number of direct-care workers will need to increase. Direct-care workers are nursing assistants, home health aides, and personal care aides who assist people in their homes. By 2022, the direct-care workforce will number 4.6

million workers, just behind retail salespeople at 4.8 million. This workforce will out-number all the K–12 teachers in the country.[19] To meet the demand, their numbers will have to increase to 2.5 million by 2030.[20]

These positions are low-paying jobs that demand the expertise and knowledge needed to help the homebound. In many cases, these jobs also require physical strength to help move people who need help bathing or going to the restroom. As we look to the future, the challenge will be in finding the number of direct-care workers that will be needed.

An article in the *Atlantic Monthly* on "Who Will Care for America's Seniors" delves into the complex concerns of direct-care workers. Issues such as diminishing Medicare payments, the goal of moving people from hospitals to homes to save costs, the diminishing potential labor pool, and the challenge of finding people to do the work, all point to the coming silver tsunami that will greatly affect the health care of boomers as they age.

Deane Beebe, spokeswoman for the Paraprofessional Healthcare Institute, says, "These are very hard jobs. They're very physically taxing—they have one of the highest injury rates of any occupation—and they're very emotionally taxing: It's intimate work; it's isolating work."[21]

Who Will Take Care of the Boomers?

Another way to get at the question of who will care for aging boomers is to look at the number of dependents over sixty-five compared to workers who are ages twenty-five to sixty-four. In 2010, there were four workers supporting one retiree. By 2040, there will be two workers per retiree.

Dowell Myers and John Pitkin from the University of Southern California have issued a number of reports about the challenges that await policy makers in Southern California when it comes to the explosion of what they call the senior dependency rate. What they say applies not only to the Los Angeles area, but to the nation as a whole.

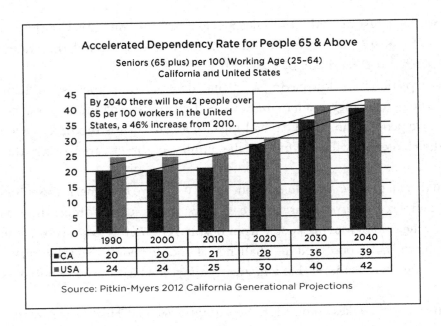

Accelerated Dependency Rate for People 65 & Above

Seniors (65 plus) per 100 Working Age (25-64)
California and United States

By 2040 there will be 42 people over 65 per 100 workers in the United States, a 46% increase from 2010.

	1990	2000	2010	2020	2030	2040
■ CA	20	20	21	28	36	39
■ USA	24	24	25	30	40	42

Source: Pitkin-Myers 2012 California Generational Projections

Increases in the senior ratio reflect the rising burdens of elderly needs placed on working age residents. This includes support for the old-age "entitlements" of pensions, Social Security, and Medicare, as well as the rising need to find adequate replacement workers for retirees. The old-age burden also includes the need to find young home buyers who can offer good prices to a rising number of older sellers. Given that older people have stored much of their wealth and retirement savings in their home equity, a substantial threat is posed by the swelling ratio of potential older sellers relative to the smaller ranks of potential homebuyers. A lot is riding on the shoulders and wallets of the new generation of young adults.[22]

As boomers move further into their second half of life, the issue of how to take care of the rising number of people who will need ongoing care will become a top political battle and cultural debate. Boomers who have families will be the fortunate ones, as they will have advocates for their treatments. Boomers who are on their own will be at the mercy of the health-care system and government services.

Churches will also play a role for those who no longer can care for themselves. Congregations that focus on creating a network of caregivers made up of families, members of the church, and people from their communities have the opportunity to create effective ministries that will benefit boomers as they age.

The Question of Death

Beyond the question of caregiving for those who suffer from a range of illnesses and conditions is the question of death itself. While most people avoid the topic, those in the funeral business are very much aware of the changes coming their way. The number of deaths in the United States will go from 2.6 million in 2015 to 3.2 million in 2030 to just over 4 million in 2050.[23]

Just as they have shaped every other industry they have touched, boomers will have an impact on funerals and funeral homes. Having been raised in the age of sitcoms, boomers do not relish the idea of going out like a scene in *Seinfeld* as the mourners dress in black, whisper snarky remarks, or listen to a pastor try to make up good things to say about someone he or she never met as dour organ music plays in the background.

Jeffrey Seeley, the vice president of strategic marketing for the Batesville Casket Company, is seeing a change in the way boomers approach the funeral. "Baby Boomers are truly shaping the funeral of the future. They're adding personal touches to make the ceremony a unique celebration of an individual's life, rather than the mourning of a death."[24]

Some funeral homes are innovating by setting up themed viewing rooms that capture the uniqueness of individuals. Rather than a parlor, some funeral homes have created theater-style sets for viewing like a kitchen or the eighteenth green at a golf course, or a family-style living room, with the idea that these sets better represent the personalities of the departed.

Funeral homes are not the only businesses aware of the commercial potential of death. On the Walmart website, customers can order their own caskets and urns that are designed to reflect the personalities and passions of the deceased. For example, you can order the Official New York Yankees Urn. Made of die-cast metal, the urn sits on a home plate, has the official team logo, and has a see-through holder that displays a baseball that can be taken out and signed by loved ones. The website says, "Ideal for home or columbarium, the urn has a screw-top lid for easy handling and holds up to 275 cubic inches of remains. It is the perfect resting place for any Bronx Bombers fan—man, woman or child."[25]

Ann Bastianelli, CEO of marketing firm Anthology Consulting and a marketing professor at Indiana University, points out the boomers' view of life is also reflected in the way they approach death. "One of the things we identified was this whole notion that your life is individual and personalized, and your death should be also."[26]

As boomers face the twin pillars of diminishing health and death, Atul Gawande in *Being Mortal* makes a powerful observation that challenges our concepts about aging and mortality. Rather than treating aging as a normal part of the life cycle, our society treats it like it's a disease.

As a doctor, Gawande had been trained to cure diseases. But as he worked with older patients, he began to question the heroic methods used on people for whom surgeries and toxic medicines would do little to cure them and make their last days of life a time of misery. He began to wonder if the treatments were more about his desire to cure someone than taking care of the needs of someone for whom these treatments did little to preserve their dignity or give them time to prepare for their deaths.

He says:

You don't have to spend much time with the elderly or those with terminal illness to see how often medicine fails the people it is supposed to help. The waning days of our lives are given over to treatments that addle our brains and sap our bodies for a sliver's chance of benefit. They are spent in institutions—nursing homes and intensive care units—where regimented, anonymous routines cut us off from all the things that matter to us in life. . . . Lacking a coherent view of how people might live successfully all the way to their very end, we have allowed our fates to be controlled by the imperatives of medicine, technology, and strangers.[27]

His observations bring home the message that American culture has a problem when it comes to taking care of the infirm and the dying. While many cultures venerate the old and families have an obligation to take care of their elderly relatives, the youth-loving Americans are not sure what to do with them.

There are a number of reasons why we are in a quandary about how to take care of the aged. First, elderly people are invisible. TV shows, movies, and advertising rarely, if ever, show a person over eighty. And if they do, it's always for comic effect. Anyone remember, "Where's the beef?"

Second, the characteristics of old age—poor eyesight, walking with a cane or walker, and slowed responses in communication—are seen as the result of illnesses that need to be cured instead of being the natural marks of old age.

Third, elderly people are segregated in nursing homes or retirement villages or are homebound by themselves or with relatives. If a young person doesn't have an elderly person in the family, he or she may not know the elderly even exist.

Because of these factors, it is almost impossible to believe in a future where we will have double the number of people in need of ongoing care and that we—the boomers—will be the people who need the care.

You would think that with the explosive growth in the numbers of aging boomers medical schools would be churning out geriatric doctors who specialize in managing the health needs of the elderly. Rather than seeing a growth in numbers, there is a decline in these specialists; some medical schools are shutting down the training completely. Because most payments to geriatric doctors are made through Medicaid or Medicare, medical students are shying away from this specialty because the pay is low.[28]

Dr. Heather Whitson, an associate professor at Duke University School of Medicine, says, "We are not prepared as a nation. We are facing a crisis. Our current health care system is ill equipped to provide the optimal care experience for patients with multiple chronic conditions or with functional limitations and disabilities."[29]

While the issues of care giving may be front and center for boomers, the issues of faith, meaning, and purpose will become more prominent as boomers move deeper into their second half of life.

Deep Change or Slow Death?

Robert E. Quinn in his book *Deep Change* wrestles with how people and organizations deal with change.[30] He says, "We live in a tumultuous time. Change is everywhere, and we are surrounded by circumstances that seem to demand more than we can deliver. We are all regularly lured into playing the role of the powerless victim or the passive observer. We look at everything in a superficial way. We see little potential and have little reverence. . . . Today, however, the dilemma is more blatant. As soon as we find meaning and equilibrium, it is distorted. We must continually choose between deep change or slow death."

Quinn expands his insights to point out that slow death is the path of least resistance. Slow death is seen in individuals and organizations when they lose trust, are experiencing burnout, and are hungry for anyone who seems to have a vision that offers hope.

He identifies three responses to slow death. First, there is *peace and pay*. Rather than make changes, the goal is to keep the status quo and to take no risks.

Second is *active exit*. A person with this mindset is looking for a way out. Instead of staying to take on the issues, a person prepares his or her resume or waits for retirement.

Third is *deep change*. People who embrace deep change are not afraid to face the current reality of their situations and become proactive about their future. As individuals, this may mean taking responsibility for their health by changing eating habits, getting more sleep, paying attention to their personal care, exercising, and connecting with other people.

That's the challenge of deep change. Most of us know there are things we can do to better our lives, but for some reason we choose the path of least resistance and choose slow death over deep change.

That is the challenge before us as we contemplate a very different future where we cannot ignore the increasing costs of taking care of those over age sixty-five. We must address the issues of what kind of care will be provided to those facing their mortality and who will take care of them. Instead of just trying to manage illness and infirmity, we must insist that people be treated as individuals who still have dreams, longings, and hopes.

Right now, it appears that slow death is winning the day. But boomers, who have faced the challenges of the past, have showed little inclination to embrace the status quo. If they choose deep change, then what is viewed as adequate care today will be transformed.

Just think, ten years ago the iPhone hadn't even been released, and tablets like the iPad had yet to be invented. When people drove to a new destination, they still used maps or printed directions off the Internet. They didn't have a turn-by-turn application that gives them real-time directions as they drive. If we had a meeting with a distant group of people, we would travel to the same location to talk rather than using GoTo-Meetings or Google Hangouts to conduct our business.

In the future, medical advances will continue to evolve to the point where treatments will be based on an individual's genetics. Medical devices disguised as robots will monitor vital signs, dispense medicines, and offer ways to get medical treatments that are unimaginable to us today. Nurse practitioners will be on the frontline of patient care, and doctors will provide expertise as needed.

We know that our current system for taking care of those at the end of their lives is inadequate for current needs and that the system will be overrun in the future if nothing changes. It will be every person for himself or herself, with those who can afford "concierge" doctors, personal direct-care givers, and state-of-the art care centers in the lead. Those who are dependent on government services and entitlements will face diminishing caregiving options, will be in competition for limited resources, and will usher in something our society thought had been regulated to history—the destitute elderly whose very lives will be dependent on the mercy of others.

The Future of Faith

The prognosticators of the 1960s imagined a secular future, where the commonsense ideas of modernity would prevail, where science would defeat superstition, and religion would be a sideshow on the world stage. Boomers who grew up in the 1950s and 1960s remember a time when the Soviet Union and China sought to abolish faith and replace it with communism.

A *Time* magazine article on April 8, 1966, "Is God Dead?" highlighted the state of religion in the 1960s. It noted that almost two-thirds of the world's population lived under governments that had condemned and—in some cases—had banned religion altogether.

Thus, it is quite a surprise to discover that rather than declining, religious faith is exploding around the world. By 2050, there will be 750 million new Christians and 1.1 billion new Muslims. Some 31.4 percent of the world's population will be Christians, and 29.7 percent will be Muslims. While the unaffiliated will add 99 million to its share of the worldwide population, the group will actually decline as a percentage of the world population from 16.4 percent in 2010 to 13.2 percent in 2050.[31]

So what is going on here? John Micklethwait and Adrian Wooldridge, in the thought-provoking book *God Is Back: How the Global Revival of Faith Is Changing the World*, make the case that religion is booming because of the remarkable success of the American model of religion versus the European model.

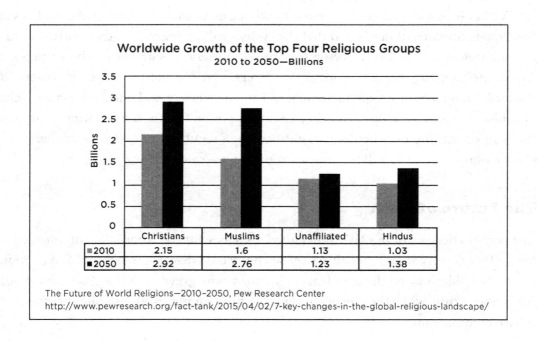

Worldwide Growth of the Top Four Religious Groups
2010 to 2050—Billions

	Christians	Muslims	Unaffiliated	Hindus
2010	2.15	1.6	1.13	1.03
2050	2.92	2.76	1.23	1.38

The Future of World Religions—2010-2050, Pew Research Center
http://www.pewresearch.org/fact-tank/2015/04/02/7-key-changes-in-the-global-religious-landscape/

The Second American Revolution

They point out that there were two American revolutions.

The first revolution was the political revolution with the eventual adoption of the United States Constitution and the Bill of Rights that formed the American style of government. The second revolution was a radical shift in the way religious institutions interacted with the government.

As the dust settled from the American Revolution, the framers of the constitution soundly rejected the European view of religion that kings and queens were the heads of their governments and their national churches. The American model separated government and religion so that governments could not control religious movements. This had an unattended consequence that now fuels the growth of religious faith. The authors state:

> In Europe established churches sided with the old regime against the new world of democracy and liberty. In America, where there was no national established church, faith embraced both democracy and the market: the only way they could survive was to attract customers. In Europe, "religion" meant war or oppression, Edmund Burke once observed: in America, it turned out to be a source of freedom.[32]

As crass as it may seem, what fueled the birth of the first church born on American shores, the Methodist Church, were the twin concepts of pluralism and competition. In Europe, you were born into a faith. If you were English, you also were a part of the Church of England. It was your birthright. In the United States, you had no religious birthright. If you wanted faith, you needed to choose it for yourself.

Because of this freedom to choose, anyone could start a religion; and if he or she attracted a crowd, it could become a religion. The concept of the religious marketplace led to a tolerance for other ways of believing or expressing one's faith. Why? You need more than one option if you want to have a choice.

Choice also leads to something else, competition. If you are going to build a religious brand, you need to outthink, out-strategize, and out-faith the other religious traditions. To get a crowd, you need to offer something that is better. The first religious group that took advantage of this new dynamic was the Methodist Church that was formed after the American Revolution in 1784.

When Francis Asbury began his work in America in 1771 there were 550 Methodists in the country, most of them followers of the English movement led by John Wesley, who saw his group as an offshoot of the Church of England.[33] After the revolution, few former colonists were interested in being part of the Church of England, so the leaders of the Methodist movement formed a church independent of the Church of England, making it the first church born in the United States.

The American Methodists employed many innovative strategies, including setting up circuits of new churches that were maintained by a circuit rider, a preacher who visited each church on a regular basis. They also started the camp meeting, which brought together large crowds of people for worship, instruction, and networking with people who were dispersed in rural areas. New converts were encouraged to be part of a small group for spiritual accountability, and music and worship services were distributed through the publishing of Methodist hymnals, collections of songs used in church services. By the time Asbury died in 1861, more than a million people, about one-eighth of the entire population of the United States, identified themselves as Methodists.[34]

The Methodist model showed the power of faith when it was unshackled from a government. Having a choice meant churches needed to create ministries that were important to the people who joined. If they did not offer vital ministry, people were free to go somewhere else. They were not obligated to stay.

Over time, churches learned to innovate and change to meet changes in the culture. Worship formats, music styles, and musical instrumentation have all changed over the years. The adoption of microphones and speakers, LCD projectors and screens, websites and live streaming of worship all came as a result of churches continually updating their technology as a way to stay relevant to the current culture.

This American concept of faith being something that a person chooses has won the day in vast stretches of the world. Across the planet, people are gravitating in record numbers to faith in God. China, whose government is still Communist, has seen an explosive growth in Christianity. In Africa, both Christians and Muslims are attracting new adherents as people discover the opportunity to choose faith. In Latin America, Catholics and Protestants are experiencing religious revival as the young embrace a belief in God.

So what does this mean for the future of faith, especially when it comes to boomers and their children and grandchildren? Churched boomers often equate faith with being a member of their church or denomination. For them, a true Christian attends worship regularly in a sanctuary, gives regularly to the church, and serves on various committees. In addition, active boomers believe that being part of a Sunday school or small group enhances faith.

What Do We Call Those Who Are Not Showing Up?

But what about those who are not participating in a church? Over the years, church leaders have come up with a number of terms to describe these people. "Unbelievers" was in vogue in the 1960s and 1970s. These were the people who did not believe in Jesus. The church's job was to convince them to believe by using tracts like the "Four Spiritual Laws" to change their minds.

In the 1980s and 1990s, the term "seekers" was used to describe people who did not come to church, but were interested in spirituality of some kind. So churches created seeker services that did not expect attendees to do anything but listen to a band play contemporary music, watch video clips, and listen to a message with fill-in-the-blank outlines. The goal was to help people become seekers of Jesus.

Now the people who do not affiliate with a particular faith tradition or go to church are called the "nones." According to Pew Research Center's recently released study on *America's Changing Religious Landscape*,[35] which reported on the rapid decrease in people who are part of mainline Protestant churches, the number of the religiously unaffiliated adults, the so-called nones, has increased by nineteen million people since 2007. Now there are approximately fifty-six million religiously unaffiliated adults in the United States, which makes them a larger group than Catholics or mainline Protestants. While 11 percent of older adults are in this category, more than 36 percent of young adults do not participate in a religious faith community.

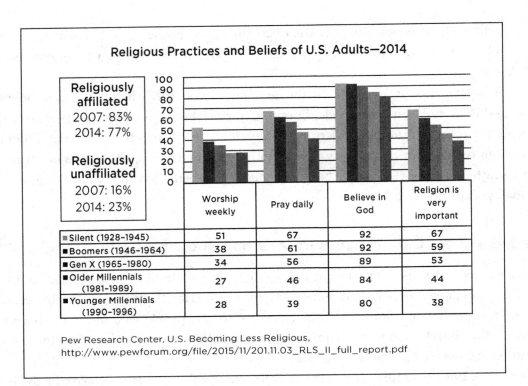

Religious Practices and Beliefs of U.S. Adults—2014

		Worship weekly	Pray daily	Believe in God	Religion is very important
Silent (1928–1945)		51	67	92	67
Boomers (1946–1964)		38	61	92	59
Gen X (1965–1980)		34	56	89	53
Older Millennials (1981–1989)		27	46	84	44
Younger Millennials (1990–1996)		28	39	80	38

Religiously affiliated
2007: 83%
2014: 77%

Religiously unaffiliated
2007: 16%
2014: 23%

Pew Research Center, U.S. Becoming Less Religious,
http://www.pewforum.org/file/2015/11/201.11.03_RLS_II_full_report.pdf

The most damning finding from the survey is that while 85 percent of adults were raised as Christians, a quarter of these no longer claim a religious affiliation. Former Christians now represent 19 percent of the U.S. population. This is more than those who identify as mainline Protestants, who have declined from 18 percent of the population to 11 percent since 2007.

In some ways, the term "nones" is a convenient term that lets the church off the hook. Church leaders can say that people aren't coming to their churches because they have lost their faith or because they don't believe in anything. But in listening to those who are unaffiliated, there may be many reasons why they have found individual churches lacking.

Instead of finding houses of worship as places of grace, some people have encountered toxic personalities they do not want their children to emulate. Or maybe preaching that constantly judges them and their friends' lifestyles as being sinful and unchristian turns them off. Or they don't understand why the churches in their area are monocultural, with one ethnicity and language group, while the rest of the world is multicultural and multilingual.

Kaya Oakes, in her intriguing book *The Nones Are Alright,* explores the stories of young people who are part of growing population of the unaffiliated in the United States. She makes the case that rather than being disinterested in God or faith or Jesus, many do not go to church precisely because people in the church are not open to the discussions and ideas about which they are so passionate. She says,

> The future of faith, however, for all of our efforts to understand it, remains a mystery. But isn't faith also a mystery? And isn't that why some of us—from the students telling us on Sproul Plaza that God loves us, to the seminarians clouded with doubt but still preparing to lead congregations, to the seekers sharing a meal—still remain drawn to faith, in its many manifestations—We may talk in church basements, on the streets, in classrooms, in living rooms. We may talk to our elders and to children at the same time. But we will talk, relentlessly, about doubt and faith and social structures, about the broken world and what we can do to repair it, about how we can be better, and what we can do to become good.[36]

So rather than connecting with the current culture in order to redeem it, churches across the United States are grappling with the question of how to reach the younger generations. They long for young people to participate in their ministries and wonder why they don't show up.

Churches Blindsided by Corporate Do-Gooders

Mainline denominations are especially challenged because most of their churches have wrapped their identities and purpose around doing social good for people in their communities. Much of their ministry revolves around providing food for the hungry, or raising money for mission work around the world, or meeting the physical needs of people in the community. The work that has been done has provided a safety net to millions of people over the years. In some communities, churches are the last remaining institution that is focused on taking care of people in their communities.

But in the last five years, a huge cultural shift has blindsided them. Virtually every business from the local grocery store to major companies like Target, Ford, and Microsoft have embraced the concept of doing social good.

I encountered this shift when talking to a group of parents of elementary school children when I said one of the most important things churches can do to attract people is to offer ministries that help people in the community. They almost laughed at me. One person said, "Are you kidding me? Every group my daughter is part of does something for the community. Even her school has its own project."

This shift in business practices can largely be credited to boomer leadership in workplaces that have discovered that business does not just have to be about making a profit. In fact, giving back to the community and doing social good is good for business. More important, younger employees want to work for companies that are doing more than just making widgets. They want what they do to have meaning and purpose. Doing good is not an option anymore; it's integral to running a successful company.

Tech and social media moguls like Bill Gates and Mark Zuckerberg have made front-page news with announcements about how they are planning to use their wealth for social good. When Mark Zuckerberg and his wife, Dr. Priscilla Chan, celebrated the birth of a baby girl, they announced they would give away 99 percent of their wealth, roughly $45 billion over the course of their lifetimes, to fund the Chan Zuckerberg Initiative to focus on "personalized learning, curing disease, connecting people and building strong communities."

In a letter written to their newborn daughter, they stated the vision for their new initiative to "advance human potential and promote equality for all children in the next generation."[37]

This new generosity is fueled by the reality that today's younger customers are not interested in buying products from companies that do not care or give back. Bill Roth, in "How Generation Z Will Make CSR a Business Norm" talks about the expectations of the youngest generation, whom he calls Generation Z, whose leading edge is just entering college. He points out if companies want to stay in business, they will have to pay attention to what is called corporate social responsibility (CSR).

He says, "Generation Z views corporate social responsibility as a core brand identifier for products and businesses. This generation rejects gender, ethnic, or sexual-preference intolerance and discrimination. . . . CSR will be this generation's foundation for evaluating what companies they will work for and do business with."[38]

As a result of the new understanding of corporate social responsibility, every retailer has its way of showing it cares. I encountered this recently when I was at the checkout counter of my local Publix grocery store. Next to the cashier were bags of groceries already prepackaged to be given to the local food bank. When the customer in front of me donated seven dollars for a bag, the cashier rang a bell, and the other cashiers and baggers all let out a cheer.

When it comes to doing good, churches are not the only game in town. While this is great for those who will be served by the desire of so many companies to do good, churches will have to reassess what they have to offer.

Churches That Will Thrive

Churches that will thrive in the future will still need to do social good, but they will need to focus on three additional essential elements: First, they will have an intentional discipleship system that teaches people the basics of the Christian faith, its beliefs, and its practices. They will encourage personal prayer, daily reading of the Bible, and being part of small groups that enable people to grow in faith. Second, they will offer spiritual experiences such as worship, prayer groups, health and spirituality retreats, and ongoing small groups that foster a deep connection to one another and to God. Third, they will be vibrant faith communities that represent the cultural mosaic of the places where they are located. These faith communities will encourage face-to-face encounters that are enhanced by vibrant social media sites that provide a spiritual connection 24/7.

Most important, they have the opportunity to create intergenerational faith communities that give the young and the old normative experiences of worshiping, praying, and learning together. Beyond the family, they are one of the few places in a community where people of different generations can interact on a regular basis. This interaction is essential for mentoring, sharing faith, and understanding for both the youngest and the oldest members of a congregation.

Boomers in churches will play a large part in this transition, as churches become spiritual centers that enhance the lives of the youngest and the oldest members of the faith community. These spiritual centers will still do good in the community and, in many cases, will be the only institution in the community that has the resources to adopt a local school or provide emergency assistance or even build senior housing or provide senior day care.

Most important, they will need to avoid the temptation to view the unaffiliated as being less Christian or spiritual than themselves. What makes them different from the unaffiliated is not necessarily faith, belief, or even a dedication to follow Jesus. What makes them different is they have been able to find a faith community that fits them, that has accepted them with all their flaws and potential, and that provides them with a safe place to explore and grow in faith.

In Pursuit of Wholeness

In today's world of instant access, there is no such thing as downtime. What we call "rest" is spent scrolling through social media sites and work-related emails to make sure we have not missed out on the latest. While previous generations could take their time to make a decision, a day seems to be too much for those who feed off the incessant streams of "likes" that seem to give life meaning.

Thinking, reflection, and contemplation seem to be words from a bygone era compared to our current reality when world events and personal requests are streamed into our brains by screens large and small that beckon to us from every nook and cranny of our existence.

Our brains were not designed for the digital world. They are not minicomputers that just happen to be housed in the upper part of our bodies. Our brains are organic. They are shaped by every sight, sound, touch, smell, and taste our body encounters.

Life as described in the first part of Psalm 23, "The Lord is my shepherd, I shall not want. He makes me lie down in green pastures; he leads me beside still waters; he restores my soul," is much more conducive to happiness than driving down a four-lane interstate trapped between two big rigs as you respond to a call on your hands-free device.

As a generation, boomers are caught in a *Back to the Future* mindset. While their children and grandchildren take the latest technological marvel as par for the course, boomers are reluctant to admit that, in many ways, they are overwhelmed. They remember dial-up phones, black and white TVs, calculators the size of a book, and TV dinners cooked in the oven, not in a microwave.

Many are happy to have mastered their device or digital workplace solution only to be told that to keep up they must learn to use the newest bit of technology. While leading-edge boomers created the first companies and products built on the World Wide Web, younger generations are far more adept at using tech gear like smartphones and tablets; and younger generations tend to be more comfortable accessing information on the Internet.

In contrast, the iKids, the generation born from 2000 to 2017, are growing up in a complex world filled with a constant flow of interactions with a wide variety of sources on a constant basis. A 2015 study by Common Sense Media discovered that tweens (ages eight to twelve) consume six hours of media a day, while teens (ages thirteen to eighteen) are on their media devices nine hours a day. When they get out of school, young people are immersed in the digital culture.[39] In many ways, they are just echoing the older millennials, those born from 1982 to 1999, who report using media devices eighteen hours a day.[40]

Of course, most boomers, especially if their work demands it, are also using the tools of the Internet to work, to connect with others, and to be informed about what is happening in the world. But there is a fundamental difference in the way boomers interact with digital media compared to the youngest generations. For boomers, the computers, smartphones, and tablets are for getting things done. For younger generations, digital media is their life.

Boomers' favorite social media site is Facebook, with approximately 56 percent participating. While many use it for work, the majority have found it to be a great way to keep up with extended family and friends. It is their digital scrapbook, where they put up pictures of celebrations, vacations, children, and grandchildren. It also is a place to ask for and receive support when someone faces a serious illness or loses a loved one.

So while there are a number of boomers involved in social media, it is important to note that 46 percent are not on Facebook and are probably not using social media at all. As the number of boomers on Facebook has grown, the younger generations are gravitating to other social media sites like Twitter and Instagram.

As the power of digital life increases, boomers as a whole will benefit from its implementation. After all, wouldn't be great in 2030 to hop into a self-driving car and not have to worry about driving? The only issue will be to make sure to enter the correct address of the location we want to go.

The reality is, boomers will always feel that they are behind when it comes to digital media because their brains were developed in an analog world where face-to-face communication was the norm, where football was played outside on real grass, where music

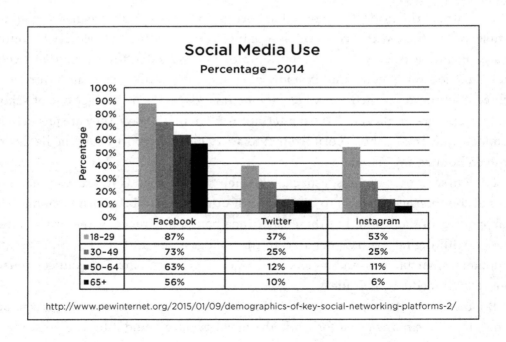

Social Media Use
Percentage—2014

	Facebook	Twitter	Instagram
▪18–29	87%	37%	53%
▪30–49	73%	25%	25%
▪50–64	63%	12%	11%
▪65+	56%	10%	6%

http://www.pewinternet.org/2015/01/09/demographics-of-key-social-networking-platforms-2/

was played on a piano in the living room, where dolls had hair to comb, and building blocks were stacked on the floor.

The iKids have brains that are being formed by playing games on five-inch screens or on game platforms that allow them to connect with competitors around the world. They don't have to walk across the street to visit their friends; they just have to turn on their smartphone and talk to them on Skype or, even better, engage in an endless conversation with 140-character text messages. They don't need to have a twenty-volume *Encyclopedia Britannica* in their home library to do their homework; they just have to Google their questions, and the answers will magically appear. They don't need to use Wite-Out when they misspell when they're typing, because the word processor will automatically correct spelling for them.

As the digital culture accelerates, boomers will also be beneficiaries. They will be able to video-chat with far-flung family members and friends. New medical devices and treatments will keep them healthy. Entertainment options will give them opportunities to explore the world from the confines of their living room.

But boomers will find themselves lost at times, especially in understanding the ways the youngest generations think, connect, and learn. The challenge will not be how to keep up, but how to stay in the conversation with the younger generations whose experience of life is so vastly different from their own.

Boomers Grew Up in a Segmented World

One of the biggest differences is that boomers grew up in a life segmented by time. There was a right time for school and a right time for play. There was a time for work and there was a time for family. There was a time to go to worship and a time to see Grandma. Today, there is little demarcation between work, family, learning, leisure, and faith. As the sophistication of our devices has increased, the distance between what we do has grown smaller. People can just as easily do work at Starbucks as they can in an office. They can call or text a friend while on an Uber ride, on a plane, or on a beach. Technology has conquered distance and time.

So wholeness is not a strategy to integrate the various elements of our lives into a manageable lifestyle. Wholeness is something different. Wholeness is a way of being.

Churches living in the past are not designed for wholeness. They are much more comfortable being an appointment on the calendar. Worship? Join us at 10:00 a.m. on Sunday. Fellowship? We have a great dinner on Wednesday nights. Prayer? The prayer group meets on Monday at 9:00 a.m. Helping others? We will stock the food pantry on Saturday at 12:00 noon, just before the ballgame.

The problem is, people don't live that way anymore. A couple of months ago, we cut the cord on cable TV and replaced it with an antenna for local programing and Hulu for streaming TV shows and movies.

In just a few short months, the way we watch TV has been completely changed. We don't wait for *Black-ish* or *Shark Tank* to come on, afraid that we will miss them if we don't turn the TV on at the right time. Now we wait until after they air, and we stream them when we are ready to watch.

Netflix and Amazon Prime don't roll out their series over the course of a couple of months; they put up all the episodes on the first day, letting the customers decide when they want to watch the shows.

Churches of the future will need to offer more than appointment-style ministries. They will need to create seamless face-to-face experiences that are enhanced by social media. What this looks like and the kind of staffing that will be needed is anyone's guess. Beyond the mechanics of offering church, churches are now encountering a different mindset among boomers and younger generations.

Those churches that come across as anti-everything will be hard-pressed to minister to a group that has tried it all and is looking for some way to make sense of what they have been through. When boomers come through the doors of a church, they already know their "sins." They know how they have fallen short. What they need is a loving place where they can begin to put their lives back together.

The presuppositions of boomers about life are much different from those of their parents' generation. They are not concerned about dress, etiquette, or even being "moral" in the traditional sense of the word. Most couples have lived together before being married or are living together now.

The sins they are dealing with are the sins of broken relationships between lovers, between parent and child, between themselves and God, between humanity and the created world. What they are looking for is wholeness.

Wholeness and the Community of Faith

Wholeness means that a person is part of a community, a community of people who care for one another, a community that offers freedom of development, the discipline of being accountable to others, and the balance of mind, body, head, and heart. Wholeness is also found as a person lives out faith in relationship to God. For the church to offer wholeness, it must be a community, not an institution.

This community is firmly based in an authentic Christian spirituality that not only talks about faith but also puts it into action. The touchstone of the community is the belief that the God who brings salvation through Jesus Christ also calls believers to share this salvation with the world. Instead of focusing on divisive labels, such as *liberal, evangelical, fundamentalist,* and *charismatic,* the spirituality of wholeness calls believers to a new Christian worldview that focuses on two things: personal faith and justice.

Personal faith is lived out in relationship to God and in relationship to the community of believers. This faith is nourished and developed through the Holy Spirit, which enables the believer to use his or her gifts for the whole body of Christ.

Justice calls the community to be accountable for its actions, to be witnesses to the world for peace and love, to bring the liberating news of Jesus to the world, to be an ethical community from which and in which right and wrong can be judged through the wisdom of God.

Rather than a mechanistic view of spirituality based on moralisms—do not drink, do not smoke, do not dance, do not pollute—wholeness is based on the organic view that life is imbued with the Spirit of God, which causes believers to be moral as a result of God working in their lives.

True spirituality is that which is in connection with God, with the creation, and with people, as believers seek to live out their lives. A complete awareness of God's presence—as seen in the created world from the flowers to the trees, from the fish to the birds of the air, from the child at play to the elderly one near death—brings to one a sense of the wholeness of life, an understanding that through God all things are formed and because of God all things have life.

As boomers reinvent the second half of life, their spirituality will inform their decisions and choices. Throughout this book, we have been reminded that the values and beliefs we hold affect the whole of our lives—relationships, work, goals, faith, and most fundamentally, our self-understanding. It is not enough just to wander through life on a yellow brick road that leads nowhere. Instead, each of us must be challenged to look anew at life and to ask, "What is my legacy?" Each of us must be challenged to willingly inquire, "God, what are you calling me to be?"

Notes

Introduction

1. U.S. Census: Table 3. Projections of the Population by Sex and Selected Age Groups for the United States: 2015 to 2060 (NP2014-T3) December 2014.

Chapter 1

1. Peter H. Brown and Steven Gaines, *The Love You Make: An Insider's Story of the Beatles* (New York: Signet Books, 1984), 97 and 104.
2. "TV's Most Memorable Moments: 9/11 Tops the List," CBSNews.com, July 11, 2012, http://www.cbsnews.com/news/tvs-most-memorable-moments-9-11-tops-the-list.
3. Henry Hurt, *Reasonable Doubt* (New York: Holt, Rinehart and Winston, 1985), 21–22.
4. Art Swift, "Majority in U.S. Still Believe JFK Killed in a Conspiracy," http://www.gallup.com/poll/165893/majority-believe-jfk-killed-conspiracy.aspx.
5. Kurt Anderson, "Hot Mood," *Rolling Stone*, May 18, 1989 (Straight Arrow Publishers, Inc. © 1988. All rights reserved. Reprinted by permission), 58.
6. Tom Shachtman, *Decade of Shocks* (New York: Poseidon, 1983), 22–30.
7. Ibid., 49–50.
8. Aimee I. Stern, "The Baby Boomers Are Richer and Older," *Business Month*, October 1987. (Reprinted with permission, *Business Month* Magazine. Copyright © 1987, by Goldhirsh Group, Inc., 38 Commercial Wharf, Boston, MA 02110), 24.
9. Ibid.

10. The Lost Decade of the Middle Class, Pew Research Center, August 22, 2012, http://www
.pewsocialtrends.org/2012/08/22/the-lost-decade-of-the-middle-class.
11. Chris Denhart, "How the $1.2 Trillion College Debt Crisis Is Crippling Students, Parents
and the Economy," *Forbes* magazine, August 7, 2013, http://www.forbes.com/sites/special
features/2013/08/07/how-the-college-debt-is-crippling-students-parents-and-the
-economy.
12. "Young Adults, Then and Now," The United States Census Bureau, https://www.census.gov
/content/dam/Census/newsroom/c-span/2015/20150130_cspan_youngadults.pdf.
13. Ben Bergman, The Breakdown blog, January 15, 2015, http://www.scpr.org/blogs/economy
/2015/01/15/17806/la-residents-need-to-make-34-an-hour-to-afford-ave/.
14. Anne Case and Angus Deaton, "Rising morbidity and mortality in midlife among white
non-Hispanic Americans in the 21st century," PNAS, http://www.pnas.org/content
/112/49/15078.full
15. "Family & Retirement: The Elephant in the Room," A Merrill Lynch Retirement Study, conducted in partnership with Age Wave, 2013, https://mlaem.fs.ml.com/content/dam/ML
/Articles/pdf/Merrill-Lynch-2013-Family-and-Retirement-Study.pdf, 6
16. Anya Kamenetz, *Generation Debt: Why Now Is a Terrible Time to Be Young* (New York:
Penguin Group, 2006), xiii.
17. Eric McWhinnie, "3 hard retirement truths facing Baby Boomers," *USA Today*, March 21,
2015
18. Laura Palmer, *Shrapnel in the Heart* (New York: Vintage Books, 1988), xiv.
19. Ibid., 12–13.
20. Ibid., 15.
21. William Greider, "Rolling Stone Survey," *Rolling Stone*, April 7, 1988, (Straight Arrow Publishers, Inc. © 1989. All rights reserved. Reprinted by permission), 36.
22. Palmer, xii.

Chapter 2

1. Kathryn A. London and Barbara Foley Wilson, "Divorce," *American Demographics*, October 1988, 23.
2. Ibid., 57.
3. Ibid.
4. David Bloom, "Childless Couples," *American Demographics*, August 1986, 23.
5. Ken Dychtwald and Joe Flower, *Age Wave* (Los Angeles: Jeremy P. Tarcher, 1989), 11.
6. David Sheff, "Portrait of a Generation," *Rolling Stone*, May 5, 1988, 49–50.
7. Craig Miller based on U.S. Census, Table A1. Marital Status of People 15 Years and Over,
by Age, Sex, Personal Earnings, Race, and Hispanic Origin/1, 2014

8. Susan Littwin, *The Postponed Generation: Why American Youth Are Growing Up Later* (New York: William Morrow and Company, Inc., 1986), 215.

9. *The United Methodist Book of Worship* (Nashville, TN: The United Methodist Publishing House, 1964), 29.

10. Sheela Kennedy and Steven Ruggles. 2014. "Breaking Up Is Hard to Count: The Rise of Divorce in the United States, 1980–2010." *Demography*, 51: 587–598.

11. "More Baby Boomers Facing Old Age Alone," Bowling Green State University News, April 16, 2012, http://www.bgsu.edu/news/2012/04/facing-old-age-alone.html.

12. Robert S. Weiss, *Loneliness: The Experience of Emotional and Social Isolation* (Cambridge, MA: MIT Press, 1973), 1.

13. Ibid., 1.

14. Ibid., 10.

15. Ibid., 14.

16. Letitia Anne Peplau and Daniel Perlman, *Loneliness: A Sourcebook of Current Theory, Research and Therapy* (New York: John Wiley, 1982), 172–74.

17. Ibid., 172.

18. Judith Waldrop, "Who Are the Caregivers?," *American Demographics*, September 1989, 39.

19. Peplau and Perlman, 172.

20. Kathleen O'Brien, "Suicide Rates Higher among Baby Boomer Men, Study Finds," *The Washington Post*, https://www.washingtonpost.com/national/religion/suicide-rates-higher-among-baby-boomer-men-study-finds/2014/08/20/ddfcaad4-287e-11e4-8b10-7db129976abb_story.html.

21. Peplau and Perlman, 172.

22. "Loneliness as an American Epidemic," *U.S. News & World Report*, July 21, 1986. Used by permission.

23. Peplau and Perlman, 172.

24. Suzanne M. Bianchi and Judith A. Seltzer, "Life without Father," *American Demographics*, December 1986. (Reprinted with permission. © American Demographics, Dec. 1986), 43.

25. Cheryl Russell, *100 Predictions for the Baby Boom* (New York: Penum, 1987), 206.

26. Peplau and Perlman, 174.

27. Susan Littwin, *The Postponed Generation* (New York: William Morrow and Company, Inc., 1986), 15–16.

28. Ibid., 16.

29. Ibid., 52.

30. Dan Kiley, *Living Together, Feeling Alone* (New York: Prentice Hall, 1989), 3.

31. Ibid., 23.

32. Ibid., 4–5.

33. Ibid., 13.

34. Weiss, 19.

Chapter 3

1. Annie Gottlieb, *Do You Believe in Magic?* (New York: Time Books, 1987), 84.
2. Midge Decter, *Liberal Parents, Radical Children* (New York: Coward, McCann & Geoghegan, 1975), 27.
3. Peter F. Drucker, *The New Realities* (New York: Harper & Row, 1989), 188–90.
4. Michael J. Weiss, *The Clustering of America* (New York: Harper & Row, 1988), 170.
5. Barbara Ehrenriech, *Fear of Falling: The Inner Life of the Middle Class* (New York: Pantheon Books, 1989), 227–28.
6. Ibid., 37.
7. Ibid.
8. Ken Dychtwald and Joe Flower, *Age Wave* (Los Angeles: Jeremy P. Tarcher, 1989), 15.
9. Ehrenriech, 92.
10. Charles Kaiser, *1968 in America* (New York: Weidenfeld & Nicolson, 1988), 191.
11. Todd Gitlin, *The Sixties: Years of Hope, Days of Rage* (New York: Bantam Books, 1987), 199.
12. Ibid., 196–201.
13. Ibid., 201.
14. Gottlieb, 169.
15. Peter Brown and Steven Gaines, *The Love You Make: An Insider's Story of the Beatles* (New York: Signet Books, 1983), 143–44.
16. Gottlieb, 175.
17. Charles Perry, *The Haight-Ashbury* (New York: Vintage Books, 1985), 122.
18. Ibid., 95.
19. Ibid., 130.
20. Gitlin, 206
21. Ibid., 205–6.
22. Brown and Gaines, 181.
23. Ibid., 222.
24. Ibid., 221.
25. "Drug Use Surges among Baby Boomers," Promises Treatment Centers, October 8, 2013, http://www.promises.com/articles/addiction/drug-use-surges-among-baby-boomers.
26. Zusha Elinson, "Aging Baby Boomers Bring Drug Habits into Middle Age," *Wall Street Journal*, March 16, 2015, http://www.wsj.com/articles/aging-baby-boomers-bring-drug-habits-into-middle-age-1426469057.
27. Ibid.
28. Ibid.
29. Studs Terkel, *The Great Divide: Second Thoughts on the American Dream* (New York: Avon Books, 1988), 334.

30. Perry, 288.
31. Gottlieb, 187.
32. Gitlin, 429.
33. "The Vote: Splintering the Great Coalition," *Time*, November 20, 1972, http://content.time .com/time/subscriber/article/0,33009,712181-3,00.html.
34. Gottlieb, 304, 312.
35. Terkel, 137–38.
36. Philip H. Dougherty, "Advertising; More Than Yuppies in Baby Boom," *The New York Times*, August 2, 1985, http://www.nytimes.com/1985/08/02/business/advertising-more -than-yuppies-in-baby-boom.html.
37. Katy Butler, "The Great Boomer Depression," *Mother Jones*, June 1989, 35.
38. Terkel, 124.
39. Walter Shapiro, "The Birth and—Maybe—Death of Yuppiedom," *Time*, April 8, 1991, 65.
40. Dougherty, "Advertising; More Than Yuppies in Baby Boom."
41. Kirk McNeill and Robert Paul, *Reaching for the Baby Boomers Workbook* (Nashville: The General Board of Discipleship of The United Methodist Church, 1989), 11-14.
42. Richard Florida, *The Rise of the Creative Class, Revisited* (New York: Basic Books, 2012), 41–56.
43. Steven Bertoni, Twinkie's Miracle Comeback: The Untold, Inside Story of a $2 Billion Feast," *Forbes*, April 15, 2015, http://www.forbes.com/sites/stevenbertoni/2015/04/15 /twinkie-billion-dollar-comeback-hostess-metropoulos-apollo-jhawar/2/.
44. Ibid.
45. "Stock Market Downturn of 2002," Wikipedia, https://en.wikipedia.org/wiki/ Stock_market_downturn_of_2002.
46. S&P/Case-Shiller U.S. National Home Price Index, Economic Research, Federal Reserve Bank of St. Louis, https://research.stlouisfed.org/fred2/series/CSUSHPINSA
47. "Value of mortgage debt outstanding in the United States from 2001 to 2015," from Statista, The Statistics Portal, http://www.statista.com/statistics/274636/combined-sum-of -all-holders-of-mortgage-debt-outstanding-in-the-us/
48. U.S. Census Bureau, "Median and Average Square Feet of floor Area in New Single-Family Houses Completed by Location," http://www.census.gov/const/C25Ann/sftotalmedav gsqft.pdf.
49. United States Census Bureau, http://www.census.gov and "2014 Foreclo- sure Filings Hit Lowest Level Since 2006, RealtyTrac Says," *Forbes*, Janu- ary 15, 2015, http://www.forbes.com/sites/erincarlyle/2015/01/15/ foreclosure-filings-drop-by-18-in-2014-hit-lowest-level-since-2006-realtytrac-says

50. Anna Clark, "Detroit Doesn't Have to Demolish Nearly as Many Homes as Planned," Next City, May 20, 2015, https://nextcity.org/daily/entry/detroit-vacant-houses-demolition-numbers-changed.

51. Mary Meehan, "The Baby Boomer Housing Bust," *Forbes* (February 21, 2014), http://www.forbes.com/sites/marymeehan/2014/02/21/the-baby-boomer-housing-bust.

52. U.S. Government Accountability Office, *Retirement Security: Most Households Approaching Retirement Have Low Savings*, May 2015, http://www.gao.gov/assets/680/670153.pdf.

53. William Grieder, "The Rolling Stone Survey: Portrait of a Generation," *Rolling Stone*, April 7, 1988, 36.

Chapter 4

1. Todd Gitlin, *The Sixties: Years of Hope, Days of Rage* (New York: Bantam Books, 1987), 424–25.

2. Susan Littwin, *The Postponed Generation* (New York: William Morrow, 1986), 24.

3. Ibid., 23.

4. Ibid.

5. *Information Please Almanac, 1990* (Boston: Houghton Mifflin, 1990), 807.

6. Midge Decter, *Liberal Parents, Radical Children* (New York: Coward, McCann & Geoghegan, 1975), 34.

7. Kenneth L. Woodward, "Young Beyond Their Years," *Newsweek Special Edition, The 21st Century Family*, Winter/Spring 1990, 55.

8. Ibid.

9. Kelly Connolly, "Allison Janney Wins Best Supporting Actress for 'Deeply Flawed' Character in *Mom*," Entertainment, September 20, 2015, http://www.ew.com/article/2015/09/20/emmys-2015-allison-janney-comedy-supporting-actress-winner-mom.

10. Peter Gray, "Declining Student Resilience: A Serious Problem for Colleges," *Psychology Today*, September 22, 2015.

11. Christopher Lasch, *The Culture of Narcissism* (New York: Warner Books, 1979), 38.

12. Ernest Becker, *The Denial of Death* (New York: Free Press, 1973), 2.

13. Michael Meyer, *The Alexander Complex* (New York: Times Books, 1989), 36–37.

14. Madonna Kolbenschlag, *Lost in the Land of Oz* (San Francisco: Harper & Row, 1988), 127.

15. Ibid., 23.

16. "Bruce Jenner: The Interview," ABC News, April 24, 2015, http://abcnews.go.com/2020/fullpage/bruce-jenner-the-interview-30471558.

Chapter 5

1. *The Yearbook of American and Canadian Churches, 2000–2010*, prepared for National Council of Churches of Christ; published by Abingdon (Nashville) and edited by Ellen Lindner. 1965, 1966 Yearbooks: Published by National Council of Churches of Christ, New York, Benson Landnis, editor.
2. Martha Farnsworth Riche, "Back to the Fifties," *American Demographics*, September 1988 (Reprinted with permission © American Demographics, Sept. 1988), 2.
3. U.S. Bureau of the Census, *Current Population Reports* Series P-25, No. 802, "Estimates of the Population of the United States."
4. "Population Change in the U.S. and the World from 1950 to 2050," ch. 4 in *Attitudes about Aging: A Global Perspective*, Pew Research Center, January 30, 2014. http://www.pew global.org/2014/01/30/chapter-4-population-change-in-the-u-s-and-the-world-from -1950-to-2050.
5. J. Ronald Oakley, *God's Country: America in the Fifties* (New York: Dembner Books, 1986), 120.
6. Ibid., 117.
7. "Percent of Population Ever Married," Department of Commerce, Bureau of the Census, 1990.
8. Wendy Wang and Kim Parker, "Never-Married Adults on the Marriage Market," ch. 4 in *Record Share of Americans Have Never Married*, Pew Research Center, September 24, 2014, http://www.pewsocialtrends.org/2014/09/24/chapter-4-never-married-young-adults -on-the-marriage-market.
9. Betty Friedan, *The Feminine Mystique, The Tenth Anniversary Edition* (New York: W. Norton, 1974), 295.
10. Sydney E. Ahlstrom, *A Religious History of the American People*, Vol. 2 (New York: Image Books, 1975), 450.
11. J. Ronald Oakley, *God's Country: America in the Fifties* (New York: Dembner Books, 1986), 323.
12. Norman Vincent Peale, *The Power of Positive Thinking* (New York: Prentice-Hall, 1952), xi.
13. Ahlstrom, 452
14. Ibid., 18.
15. Leonard I. Sweet, "The Modernization of Protestant Religion in America," *Altered Landscapes: Christianity in America*, 1935–1985 (Grand Rapids: William B. Eerdmans, 1989), 24.
16. Ibid., 30.

17. Ahlstrom, 461.
18. Sweet, 30–31.
19. Tom Wolfe, "The Me Decade and the Third Great Awakening," *The Purple Decades* (New York: Berkeley Books, 1982), 282.
20. "The Jesus Movement Is upon Us," *Look*, February 9, 1971, 15.
21. Chuck Smith and Tal Brooke, *Harvest* (Old Tappan, NJ: Chosen Books, 1987), 48.
22. Smith, 15–16.
23. Chellis Glendinning, *Waking Up in the Nuclear Age* (New York: Beech Tree Books, William Morrow, 1987), 81.
24. Hal Lindsey, *The Late Great Planet Earth*, (Zondervan, 1970), 102.
25. Ibid., 126–27.
26. Ibid., 167.
27. "'Left Behind' authors join Maddow," NBCNews.com, http://www.nbcnews.com/id/29496421.
28. "The Gold Rush to Golgotha," *Time*, October 25, 1971, 65.

Chapter 6

1. AQUARIUS/LET THE SUNSHINE IN J. Rado, J. Ragni, G. MacDermot & N. Shapiro Copyright © 1966, 1967, 1968, 1970 JAMES RADO, JEROME RAGNI, GALT MACDERMOT, NAT SHAPIRO, UNITED ARTISTS MUSIC CO., INC. All Rights Controlled by UNITED ARTISTS MUSIC CO., INC. All Rights of UNITED ARTISTS MUSIC CO., INC. Assigned to EMI CATALOGUE PARTNERSHIP All Rights Administered by EMI U CATALOG. International Copyright Secured. Made in U.S.A. All Rights Reserved.
2. Theodore Roszak, *The Making of a Counter Culture* (New York: Doubleday, 1968), 229.
3. Robert L. Johnson, "Protestant Hangups with the Counter·Culture," *The Christian Century*, November 4, 1970, 1318–319.
4. Frank Trippett, "The Hesse Trip," *Look*, February 23, 1971, 56.
5. Tom Wolfe, "The Me Decade and the Third Great Awakening," *The Purple Decades* (New York: Berkeley Books, 1982), 280.
6. George Gallup Jr. and Jim Castelli, *The People's Religion* (New York: Macmillan, 1990), 13.
7. Russell Chandler, *Understanding the New Age* (Dallas: Word, 1988), 60–61.
8. "Religion: Brainwashing Moonies," *Time*, Monday, April 4, 1977, http://content.time.com/time/subscriber/article/0,33009,947875,00.html.
9. Chandler, 61.
10. Bob Sipchen and Jonathan Weisman, "Harmonic Convergence: A Braver New World?" *Los Angeles Times*, Wednesday, August 12, 1987, Part V, 4.
11. "A New Age Dawning," *Time*, August 31, 1987, 63.

12. "New Age Harmonies," *Time*, December 7, 1987. (Copyright © 1987 Time Warner Inc. Reprinted by permission), 62.

13. John Naisbitt and Patricia Aburdene, *Megatrends 2000* (New York: William Morrow, 1990), 293.

14. Lillie Wilson, "The Aging of Aquarius," *American Demographics*, September 1988. (Reprinted with permission. © American Demographics September 1988), 34.

15. Suzanne Doucet, "Success Has Diluted New Age Music," *Billboard*, June 18, 1988 (© 1988 BPI Communications, Inc. Used by permission from Billboard), 9.

16. Chandler, 20.

17. "10 Personal Prayers That Will Get You through Anything," *Supersoul Sunday*, http://www.oprah.com/supersoulsunday/Personal-Prayers-That-Will-Get-You-Through-Anything-Video#ixzz3qKbJsDYR.

18. Russell Chandler, "Customer Poll Shapes a Church," *Los Angeles Times*, December 11, 1989, A1 and A28–A31.

19. Bruce L. Bugbee, *Networking*, Fuller Institute, Pasadena, CA.

20. Willow Creek Association, https://www.willowcreek.com/events/leadership/why_rsp.asp.

21. Rick Warren, *The Purpose Driven Church: Growth without Compromising Your Message and Mission* (Grand Rapids: Zondervan, 1995).

22. Rick Warren, *The Purpose Driven Life: What on Earth Are You Here For?* (Grand Rapids: Zondervan, 2002), 17.

23. GCFA Data Services, http://www.umc.org/gcfa/data-services.

24. Hartford Institute for Religion Research, "2012 Profile of Total North American Mega-churches," http://hirr.hartsem.edu/megachurch/megastoday_profile.html.

25. Greg L. Hawkins and Cally Parkinson, *Reveal: Where Are You?*, Willow Creek Association, 3.

26. Ibid, 57.

27. "Clergy Age Trends in the United Methodist Church: 1985–2015," Lewis Center for Church Leadership, 2015 Report, http://www.churchleadership.com/pdfs/ClergyAgeTrends15.pdf.

Chapter 7

1. *Global Age Watch Index 2015: Insight Report* (London: HelpAge International, 2015), http://reports.helpage.org/global-agewatch-index-2015-insight-report.pdf.

2. Ibid.

3. Nielson and Boomagers, "Boomers: Marketing's Most Valuable Generation," The Nielsen Company & Boomeragers, 2012, 15.

4. Bill Gifford, *Spring Chicken: Stay Young Forever (Or Die Trying)* (New York: Grand Central, 2016), 4.

5. Annie Lowrey, "Can Oprah Save Weight Watchers?" *Daily Intelligencer*, http://nymag.com /daily/intelligencer/2015/10/can-oprah-save-weight-watchers.html.

6. International Health Racquet & Sportsclub Association http://www.ihrsa.org.

7. "Boomers to Gen X and Y: Run Faster," *MarketWatch*, September 20, 2013, http://blogs .marketwatch.com/encore/2013/09/20/boomers-to-gen-x-and-y-run-faster/.

8. *An Aging Nation: The Older Population in the United States*, U.S. Census Bureau, https:// www.census.gov/prod/2014pubs/p25-1140.pdf.

9. "Children in U.S. Immigrant Families," Migration Policy Institute, http://www.migration policy.org/programs/data-hub/charts/children-immigrant-families

10. Anh Do, "Not Your Grandmother's Little Saigon: Entrepreneurs Expand Enclave's Horizons," *Los Angeles Times*, November 25, 2015.

11. Jasmine Rose Smothers and F. Douglas Powe Jr., *Not Safe for Church: Ten Commandments for Reaching New Generations* (Nashville: Abingdon, 2015) xii-xiv.

12. Ibid., 2-3.

13. "Statistical Resources," The United Methodist Church, http://www.umc.org/gcfa/data -services-statistics.

14. IHS, Inc., *The Complexities of Physician Supply and Demand: Projections from 2013 to 2025; Final Report*, Association of Medical Colleges, Washington, DC, 2015, https://www .aamc.org/download/426242/data/ihsreportdownload.pdf.

15. Lenny Bernstein, "U.S. Faces 90,000 Doctor Shortage by 2025, Medical School Association Warns," *Washington Post*, March 3, 2015, https://www.washingtonpost.com/news/to-your -health/wp/2015/03/03/u-s-faces-90000-doctor-shortage-by-2025-medical-school -association-warns/.

16. "2016 Alzheimer's Disease Facts and Figures," Alzheimer's Association, http://www.alz .org/facts.

17. Donald Redfoot, Lynn Feinberg, and Ari Houser, "The Aging of the Baby Boom and the Growing Care Gap: A Look at Future Declines in the Availability of Family Caregivers," Insight on the Issues, AARP Public Policy Institute, http://www.aarp.org/content/dam /aarp/research/public_policy_institute/ltc/2013/baby-boom-and-the-growing-care-gap -insight-AARP-ppi-ltc.pdf.

18. Angelo, Volandes, "Dying, Demented, and Alone," *Huffington Post*, April 15, 2015, http:// www.huffingtonpost.com/angelo-volandes/dying-demented-and-alone_b_7036018.html.

19. "Occupational Projections for Direct-Care Workers 2012–2022," PHI FactSheet, http:// phinational.org/sites/phinational.org/files/phi-factsheet14update-12052014.pdf.

20. "US Needs 2.5 Million More Long-Term Care Workers by 2030, Study Says," United Healthcare, http://www.uhc.com/bmtn-categories/bmtn-news/2015/06/11/us-needs -25-million-more-longterm-care-workers-by-2030-study-says.

21. Alana Semuels, "Who Will Care for America's Seniors?" *The Atlantic Monthly*, April 27, 2015, http://www.theatlantic.com/business/archive/2015/04/who-will-care-for-americas -seniors/391415/.

22. The Generational Future of Los Angeles: Projections to 2030 and Comparisons to Recent Decades, https://www.usc.edu/schools/price/research/popdynamics/futures/2013_Myers -Pitkin_LA-Projections.pdf.

23. "Table 1. Projections of the Population and Components of Change for the United States: 2015 to 2060," Population Projectons from the United States Census Bureau," https://www .census.gov/population/projections/data/national/2014/summarytables.html.

24. "Baby Boomers Want Funerals That Celebrate, Not Mourn, Batesville Casket Company Survey Shows," PR Newswire, October 9, 2000, http://www.prnewswire.com/news -releases/baby-boomers-want-funerals-that-celebrate-not-mourn-batesville-casket -company-survey-shows-74834252.html.

25. Walmart website, http://www.walmart.com/ip/Official-Major-League-Baseball-Urn -New-York-Yankees/38042516.

26. Martha White, NBC News, "Funeral Directors Thinking Outside the Box for Baby Boomers," http://www.cnbc.com/id/100788587.

27. Atul Gawande, *Being Mortal* (New York: Picador, 2015), 9.

28. Ibid., 45.

29. Magaly Olivero, "Doctor Shortage: Who Will Take Care of the Elderly?" *U.S. News and World Report*, April 21, 2015, http://health.usnews.com/health-news/patient-advice /articles/2015/04/21/doctor-shortage-who-will-take-care-of-the-elderly.

30. Robert E. Quinn, *Deep Change: Discovering the Leader Within* (San Francisco: Jossey-Bass, 1996), xiii

31. "The Future of World Religions—2010–2050," Pew Research Center, http://www.pew research.org/fact-tank/2015/04/02/7-key-changes-in-the-global-religious-landscape.

32. John Micklethwait and Adrian Wooldridge, *God Is Back: How the Global Revival of Faith Is Changing the World* (New York: Penguin Press, 2009), 9.

33. Ibid., 21–22.

34. Ibid., 21.

35. "America's Changing Religious Landscape," Pew Research Center, May 12, 2015, http:// www.pewforum.org/2015/05/12/americas-changing-religious-landscape.

36. Kaya Oakes, *The Nones are Alright: A New Generation of Believers, Seekers, and Those In Between* (New York: Orbis Books, 2015), 198.

37. Mark Zuckerberg, "A Letter to Our Daughter," Facebook, December 1, 2015.
38. Bill Roth, "How Generation Z Will Make CSR a Business Norm," TriplePundit, November 3, 2015, http://www.triplepundit.com/2015/11/generation-z-will-make-csr-business-norm.
39. "The Common Sense Census: Media Use by Tweens and Teens" Infographic, Common Sense Media, 2015, https://www.commonsensemedia.org/the-common-sense-census -media-use-by-tweens-and-teens-infographic.
40. Ipsos Media CT, Crowdtap, http://go.crowdtap.com/socialinfluence.

CPSIA information can be obtained
at www.ICGtesting.com
Printed in the USA
FSOW03n1929170917
38768FS

9 780881 777819